Goodreads review

'   ok was an absolute thrill to get, and will be so very useful
y years to come. For those who are huge Dickens lovers,
this is a must-have."

Julie, *Goodreads*

MR. CHARLES DICKENS'S LAST READING.

Who's Who in
Charles
Dickens

C. P. VLIELAND

Matador
9 Priory Business Park,
Wistow Road, Kibworth Beauchamp,
Leicestershire. LE8 0RX
Tel: (+44) 116 279 2299
Email: books@troubador.co.uk
Web: www.troubador.co.uk/matador

ISBN 9781788036184

British Library Cataloguing in Publication Data.
A catalogue record for this book is available from the British Library.

Typeset in 11pt Aldine401 BT Roman by Troubador Publishing Ltd, Leicester, UK
Printed and bound by CPI Group (UK) Ltd, Croydon, CR0 4YY

Matador is an imprint of Troubador Publishing Ltd

In memory of my father

WHO'S WHO IN CHARLES DICKENS

This book presents in compact form, possibly for the first time this century, a register of the characters in the fiction of Charles Dickens.

It presents those men and women (children, too) who either promote or enrich the action: it is aimed at Eng.Lit. students, researchers, quizmasters and others who want to find answers quickly.

Other works in this genre often take in too many walkers-on, which can make for clutter. This is a concise register, with an alphabetical list for each work in which any character can be found in a moment.

This approach has the additional advantage that, in checking on the fortunes of any particular actor, various strands of narrative are separated, allowing for greater insight into (and enjoyment of) the structure of the plot – which helps, given the complexity of many of the stories.

People are presented in Dickens's own words, with no "literary" explanations, exegesis or value judgements. It is Dickens face-to-face, a work of reference.

It is my hope that by making so many plain facts easily available it will further stimulate interest in his genius and promote pleasure in the store of riches he gave the world.

C.P.V. Sussex 2017

CONTENTS

THE KEY

Work	Code	Number of characters	Page
Tale of Two Cities, A	TAL	10	148
Selected short works			155
Chimes, The	CHIM	1	157
Christmas Carol, A	CAROL	3	158
Cricket on the Hearth, The	CRI	2	159

Total of listed characters: 212

THE DICKENS REGISTER

Character	Work	Page
Nickleby, Kate, bait for lechers?	NICK	104
Nickleby, Nicholas, go-ahead hero	NICK	105
Nickleby, Ralph, cunning usurer	NICK	107
Nickleby, Mrs, vacuous mother	NICK	108
Noggs, Newman, secret aide	NICK	108
Nubbles, Christopher (Kit), staunch friend	OCS	115
Pancks, slum busybody	DOR	81
Pecksniff, Seth, arch-hypocrite	CHUZ	91
Pecksniff, Charity, ugly sister	CHUZ	93
Pecksniff, Mercy, ugly sister	CHUZ	93
Peerybingle, John, over-loving husband	CHIM	159
Peggotty, Clara, lifelong support	DAV	33
Peggotty, Dan'el, has a mission	DAV	33
Pickwick, Samuel, genial traveller	PIC	140
Pinch, Tom, pure good nature	CHUZ	94
Pip, has Great Expectations	EXPECT	55
Plummer, Bertha, dolls' dressmaker	CHIM	159
Pocket, Herbert, Pip's good friend	EXPECT	60
Pocket, Matthew, Pip's tutor	EXPECT	61
Podsnap, Georgiana, naïve heiress	OMF	129

Character	Work	Page
Podsnap, John, "ENGLAND!"	OMF	130
Pross, Miss, fiery protectress	TAL	154
Pumblechook, silliest uncle	EXPECT	61
Quilp, Daniel, bundle of spite	OCS	115
Rigaud, French adventurer	DOR	82
Riderhood, Roger, hate-filled waterman	OMF	130
Rokesmith, John, hero incognito	OMF	130
Rouncewell, Mrs, faithful housekeeper	BLEAK	20
Rouncewell, ironmaster son	BLEAK	21
Rouncewell, George, soldier son	BLEAK	21
Rudge, Barnaby, innocent pawn	BAR	6
Rudge, Mary, ever-patient mother	BAR	7
Rudge, double murderer	BAR	7
Single Gentleman, agent for redemption	OCS	115
Scrooge, Ebenezer, seasonal icon	CAROL	158
Sikes, Bill, bad life, bad end	OLI	119
Skewton, The Hon. Mrs, scheming mother	DOM	48
Skimpole, Harold, sad hanger-on	BLEAK	22
Slyme, Chevy, crooked nephew	CHUZ	95
Smike, Dotheboys victim	NICK	109

Character	Work	Page
Twemlow, Melvin, diffident at dinner	OMF	133
Twist, Oliver, a hero survives	OLI	119
Varden, Gabriel, big-hearted locksmith	BAR	8
Varden, Dolly, jolly daughter	BAR	9
Veek, Trotty, errand-boy has dreams	CHIM	157
Veneering, Hamilton, MP with "friends"	OMF	133
Verisopht, Lord Frederick, spineless aristo	NICK	112
Vholes, the man in black	BLEAK	26
Wade, Miss, bitter spinster	DOR	83
Wardle, Mr, genial host	PIC	144
Wegg, Silas, scheming balladeer	OMF	134
Weller, Sam, faithful valet	PIC	144
Weller, Tony, coachman and counsellor	PIC	145
Wemmick, clerk with a heart	EXPECT	62
Westlock, John, friend and suitor	CHUZ	97
Wickfield, Agnes, more than a confidante	DAV	35
Wilfer, Bella, heroine in the making	OMF	135
Wilfer, Runty, long-suffering father	OMF	136
Willet, Joe, goes for a soldier	BAR	9
Willet, John, Maypole publican	BAR	10

Character	*Work*	*Page*
Winkle, Nathaniel, Pickwickian	PIC	146
Woodcourt, Dr Allan, hero at last	BLEAK	26
Wrayburn, Eugene, key barrister	OMF	136
Wren, Jenny, dolls' dressmaker	OMF	138

Total of listed characters: 212

THE NOVELS

For ease of reference, the roman numeral after a character indicates the chapter in which that character first appears.

*★★★ **(NAME IN BOLD)** indicates a pivotal character*

BARNABY RUDGE

CHESTER, EDWARD (I), dark-haired Protestant "gallant gentleman" aged about 28, loves Emma Haredale, a Catholic girl. Family opposition to the match leads him to emigrate; he stays for five years in the West Indies, where his affairs prosper; he is back in London at the time of the anti-Catholic riots in 1780 and rescues from the mob Emma's uncle, Geoffrey Haredale, who is now reconciled to the marriage; Edward takes Emma to the West Indies and they have a large family.

CHESTER, JOHN (X), Edward's father, grave man with urbane manner but "false and hollow" character, is against his son's love for Emma Haredale as he wants Edward to marry money and also because the girl is a Catholic. At the Maypole tavern he meets Emma's uncle Geoffrey Haredale and the two men agree the romance must end. Edward protests; his father banishes him; he goes abroad.

By 1780 Chester is a knight and an MP supporting the Protestant cause in Parliament. He wears the blue cockade of the Protestant Association and manipulates Lord George Gordon and his followers towards mischief without being involved himself.

After the riots, the locksmith Gabriel Varden comes to Chester in his Temple chambers and tells him that he learnt in prison that Maypole Hugh is the son of a gypsy who was seduced and abandoned by a gentleman; Sir John is therefore Hugh's natural father. Chester takes it all, literally, with a pinch of snuff.

Later that summer he meets Haredale in the ruins of his home, the Warren, and taunts him. They fight a duel; Chester is killed.

★★★DENNIS THE HANGMAN (XLIX), sadistic professional executioner, joins the Protestant Asssociation and becomes a riot leader. When the tide turns against the rioters, he betrays Hugh, Barnaby and Barnaby's father – who had been freed from Newgate by the mob – to the soldiers in the hope of escaping the noose himself, which he does not.

★★★GORDON, LORD GEORGE (XXXV), instigator of the riots subsequently named after him, arrives unexpectedly at the Maypole inn in March 1780 with two companions. He is slender, of middle height, with sallow complexion and reddish-brown hair.

His obsequious secretary, Gashford, praises a speech he has made at a Protestant rally in Suffolk and flatters everything he does; Gordon himself says it is a proud thing to lead the people even though in Parliament they "cough and jeer and groan"; his servant Grueby reflects: "my lord's half off his head". Gordon sacks Grueby when he tells his employer that local follower Barnaby Rudge is mad.

Gordon is president of what he terms the Great Protestant Association of England, which whips up public feeling against a Catholic Emancipation Bill before the House of Commons.

On 2 June 1780 he leads a mob to Westminster, where the Protestant petition he has organised is presented in the Commons and roundly rejected. The riotous crowd, led by Maypole Hugh and the naïve Barnaby, turns nasty and – spurred by Gashford who plies the leaders with liquor – loots Catholic chapels. Gashford also directs part of the mob to the Warren: the mansion is ransacked.

When the rioters are crushed Gordon is taken to the Tower of London. Years later he dies in Newgate.

HAREDALE, GEOFFREY (XI), "squarely-built, rough and abrupt in manner", meets John Chester in 1775 and agrees his niece Emma should not marry Chester's son; when Edward comes to call at Haredale's mansion, the Warren near Epping, the uncle roughly forbids him the house.

In 1780, as the anti-Catholic tension builds, Haredale, himself a Catholic, upbraids Gordon's secretary Gashford for being a turncoat.

Days later Haredale goes to see the home the mob has destroyed and sees the gaunt man among the ruins: he seizes him, calls out "You, Rudge, double murderer and monster!" He takes him to London and his captive is put into Newgate.

At the height of the riots Haredale is in danger of being lynched; he is given sanctuary by a sympathiser but is nonetheless recognised by mob leader Maypole Hugh and called out. Seeking refuge in an underground passage he is met by Edward Chester and Joe Willet and led to safety.

He meets Edward again and admits he was wrong to forbid the match with Emma. Visiting the Warren left desolate by the rioters, he meets Sir John Chester, patronising and reproachful as ever. The two men fight a duel. Chester is killed. Haredale goes abroad and enters a monastery.

★★★HUGH (XI), or "Maypole Hugh", rough-looking black-haired swarthy hostler at the inn, meets Dolly Varden in Epping forest and while making a pass at her steals from her Emma's letter to Edward and a bracelet, which he brings to Edward's father.

In 1780 Hugh becomes a fanatical supporter of the Protestant protests and is among the leaders in the mass march on the Commons. He flees to a tavern, where Gordon's secretary Gashford plies him and other riot leaders with liquor and incites them to go further: that evening Catholic chapels are looted and burned; Hugh then leads a mob which ransacks the Maypole inn; inflamed by liquor the mob burns down the Warren.

Newgate prison is invaded and the inmates freed, Hugh always to the fore. A large area of Holborn is destroyed.

The army is called out and Hugh is taken and condemned. He is fatalistic: his mother, having been seduced by John Chester and fallen on hard times, was hanged; now he faces the same fate.

His half-brother Edward Chester comes to see him buried.

MIGGS (VII), spiteful, mean-minded and "of a sharp and acid visage," maidservant to Mrs Varden, always seeking to make mischief between wife and husband, in which she fails because of Gabriel Varden's endless good nature; professes a hatred of men but has an unrequited passion for Tappertit ("What will become of me? Where is my Simmuns?") and supports his riot activity; when order is restored, the Vardens dismiss her.

★★★RUDGE, BARNABY (III), 23 years old in 1775, red-haired, sturdily built but his face reflecting "wildness and vacancy"; his green clothes bespeaking the "disorder of his mind"; his hat is decorated with limp peacock feathers. He has a pet raven called Grip, which he keeps in a basket strapped to his back.

When his mother decides to renounce the pension she has been receiving from Haredale – she has been threatened by her husband – she and her son leave and live quietly in the country for five years until they are dunned for money and flee back to London.

They reach Westminster on 2 June 1780, the day of a mass demonstration at which Lord George Gordon is to present his anti-Catholic petition to Parliament. Barnaby meets Maypole Hugh and Simon Tappertit in the crowd, gets caught up in the tumult and frenzy and, much to his mother's dismay, is naively elated to be allowed to carry a banner to Parliament.

The authorities take charge; a squadron of Foot Guards arrest Barnaby and he is thrown into a Newgate dungeon, where he meets the gaunt man and accuses him of being the robber who attacked young Chester five years before. The gaunt man replies: "I am your father." Barnaby embraces him.

Barnaby and his father are both freed when the mob sacks Newgate. He is rearrested when he and Hugh are betrayed by Dennis the Hangman; he is sentenced to die for his part in the unrest.

Gabriel Varden tries everything to get him released and gets to approach the Prince of Wales; Barnaby gets a free pardon and is reunited with his mother. They go on to make a new life on the Maypole farm, Grip the raven still in attendance.

RUDGE, MARY (V), lives with her son Barnaby in a poor house in Southwark; her face of patient composure cannot hide past suffering: the boy was born the day it became known that her husband disappeared and became a murderer on the run.

She always shielded him even though he came out of hiding in intervals to dun her for money. Her main concern is to protect "my idiot son."

The gaunt elderly man with ill-favoured features *(the reader learns later he is her husband)* visits her twice. Much distressed, she flees with her son to a country town for five years until an old acquaintance chases them for money. They flee to London which they reach just as the demonstration to Parliament is getting under way in June 1780 and Barnaby gets embroiled.

After Barnaby is pardoned he and his mother find peace working on the Maypole farm.

RUDGE, murderer of squire Reuben Haredale and a manservant in the Warren mansion in 1753 and in hiding in and around the mansion ever since, appears in his own right only three-quarters of the way through the story when Geoffrey Haredale finds him among the mansion's ruins and names him. Before that, Rudge, Barnaby's father, is always identified either as a ghost or else as the gaunt severe man of 60 with unwashed face and slouched hat; he made sporadic appearances from the start, including:

(i) In the opening chapter he is the surly man in the Maypole inn who hears Solomon Daisy tell the story of the Warren murder (and wrongly identifying the murdered servant as Rudge, so confusing victim with perpetrator), on the same night upsetting Gabriel Varden and robbing Edward Chester;

(ii) Makes calls on his wife mainly for money; she never gives him away but at one stage flees London to be rid of him;

(iii) Forces the blind man Stagg, who has at times acted as his intermediary, into giving him shelter for a night;

(iv) After the Warren is burned down, Geoffrey Haredale finds him, calls him out by his name and delivers him to justice.

Rudge is confined to Newgate and there finds his son Barnaby – who embraces him. He and his son are freed from Newgate when the rioters sack the prison. Rudge is retaken by soldiers on the last night of the unrest and hanged.

***TAPPERTIT, SIMON (IV)**, Gabriel Varden's apprentice, small-eyed, 5ft tall, vain, and with tremendous self-regard boosted by his leadership of a secret society called the "Prentice Knights", young men who rail against their "Tyrant Masters". They meet in a dirty cellar owned by blind man Stagg, who is also a contact for the refugee murderer Rudge.

In 1780 the "Prentice Knights" have renamed themselves the United Bulldogs, ardent supporters (with Tappertit to the fore) of the Protestant movement of Lord George Gordon. Tappertit is one of the leaders of the march and after it is dispersed by the authorities he gets drunk, insults Gabriel Varden and flees.

He comes back with a mob to force the locksmith to help open the great door of Newgate, which Varden stoutly refuses to do. The prison defences are nevertheless breached and the mob streams in, freeing prisoners, Barnaby among them. Tappertit has taken Emma Haredale and Dolly Varden prisoner and confined them in a secret hiding place. They are rescued by Edward Chester and Joe Willet. Tappertit is seized by the soldiers. When he is released he is helped by the compassionate Varden to set up as a shoeblack.

***VARDEN, GABRIEL (II)**, cheerful red-faced locksmith with a plump and comfortable figure, is on his way to London from Epping when he comes across a horseman riding recklessly. The gaunt surly stranger is unwilling to admit his mistake and threatens him before riding off.

Some miles further on, Gabriel's coach comes across a young man robbed and wounded who is being looked after by a local passer-by, Barnaby Rudge. Varden takes charge and the victim, Edward Chester, is taken to the Rudge home.

Varden returns home to his locksmith's shop in Clerkenwell. He is always sunny and even-tempered even though his wife Martha berates him continuously with the support of her maid Miggs.

In 1780 Varden has become a sergeant in the army reserves and opposes the Gordon movement which his wife and servant support.

After the anti-Catholic demonstration Tappertit gets drunk, returns to the Vardens' home and despite Gabriel's good-natured efforts to calm him down flees into the night.

Gabriel is seized by the mob and escorted to Newgate to seek to open the door which he refuses to do. He is injured in the unrest.

When Barnaby is sentenced to hang, he does all he can to save him, eventually reaching the Prince of Wales, and through this intercession Barnaby is pardoned.

His happy daughter Dolly and Joe Willet celebrate their wedding at his home.

VARDEN, DOLLY (IV), with sparkling eyes, "the very personification of good humour and blooming beauty", is very close to her father but is loyal to her nagging mother. She loves Joe Willet of the Maypole but plays hard to get.

Edward Chester uses her to get a letter to Emma but Dolly is waylaid by Maypole Hugh on her way back and Hugh steals Emma's reply.

By 1780 she is plumper but jolly and blooming as ever; she has rejected many suitors. But when Joe comes back from America she confesses she has always loved him. They marry and take over the Maypole.

WILLET, JOE (I), aged 20 in 1775, helps his father, Maypole landlord John, in the business. He has a mind of his own and he resents his father treating him like a child; he is in love with Dolly Varden, daughter of locksmith Gabriel.

His father's bullying becomes too much. He runs away from home and enlists as a soldier.

Five years later he is back, having lost an arm in the wars in America. He describes himself as "a poor, maimed, discharged soldier" but acquits himself so well in helping to put down the riots that he is sent a silver snuff-box by the king.

Dolly Varden readily accepts him; they take over the restored Maypole inn and have many children.

WILLET, JOHN (I), long-serving landlord of the venerable Maypole inn in Epping forest near Chigwell, is burly, fat-faced, pigheaded.

On the evening in 1775 that the novel begins, parish clerk Solomon Daisy tells the bar's regulars, with John Willet presiding, that on 19 March 1753, exactly 22 years ago to the day, local squire Reuben Haredale and his servant were murdered; the perpetrators were never found.

John becomes ever more domineering over his son Joe, who eventually rebels and flees.

The story moves on to 1780. Late one night in March three horsemen unexpectedly seek accommodation at the Maypole: Lord George Gordon, his secretary Gashford and servant John Grueby.

A little later, rumours of the London riots reach him and John stoutly denies even that they are happening. He is rudely surprised when his own hostler Hugh leads a mob which ransacks his tavern, drains it of drink and ties him up before going on to destroy the Warren.

Willet is dispossessed and dies without ever coming to terms with his loss. His son Joe and daughter-in-law Dolly take over the tavern.

BLEAK HOUSE

The heroine, Esther Summerson, is the child of a woman who goes up in the world (as she marries Baronet Dedlock) and a soldier, Captain Hawdon, who goes down (as he becomes a lawyers' drudge and a drug addict).The reader is gradually made aware of this before Esther herself is.

★★★BUCKET, INSPECTOR (XXII), a middle-aged "stoutly-built, steady-looking, sharp-eyed" detective, is called in by lawyer Tulkinghorn to hear crossing-sweeper Jo's encounter with the veiled woman (whom the reader knows is Lady Dedlock).

Bucket goes to the slum where Jo lives and brings him back to Tulkinghorn's, where the lawyer has dressed the dismissed French maid Hortense in Lady Dedlock's clothes. Jo indentifies the clothes, *not* the wearer; Tulkinghorn, not averse to doing some detecting of his own, is satisfied he has discovered that the mystery woman was his own client, Lady Dedlock.

Bucket comes across Jo again when he is being sheltered by Esther at Bleak House and tells him to get away not less than 40 miles from London. The frightened boy takes to the streets again.

Tulkinghorn is found murdered. Bucket, knowing the ex-soldier Trooper George Rouncewell had ample reason to detest him, arrests him for murder.

Bucket reveals to Sir Leicester that his wife had an affair (before she was married) with Hawdon and that there was a child born of this liaison. He adds that a woman "in a loose black mantle with a deep fringe" was seen on the stairs of Tulkinghorn's chambers that night. Tulkinghorn is the family lawyer. Sir Leicester goes pale.

With a sense of theatre, Bucket next produces in Sir Leicester's own drawing room the Dedlocks' dismissed French maid Hortense and tells the baronet that she was the killer.

He says that as for women in voluminous cloaks seen at Tulkinghorn's that night, Lady Dedlock was one and Hortense was the other – because Hortense was anxious to cast suspicion on her former employer. Also on the stairs just then (to pay a debt) was Trooper George.

Bucket goes on: a pond was dragged and the murder weapon found which could only have been thrown there by Hortense. He formally stages her arrest to impress Sir Leicester and, hurling insults, Hortense is taken away.

Lady Dedlock goes missing. Bucket is ordered by Sir Leicester to find her. He calls in the help of her daughter Esther and has his police colleagues circulate the missing woman's description. The young doctor Allan Woodcourt joins the search; Lady Dedlock is found dead in the graveyard where the father of her child lies buried.

CARSTONE, RICHARD (III), about 19, ward of court in the Jarndyce court case, comes to live at Bleak House. Insouciant, charming to everyone; three attempts at a career (in medicine, law, the army) all fail because of "instability of character". He is in love with, and secretly marries, the other Jarndyce ward of court, Ada Clare.

Swayed by Skimpole's baleful influence and continually drained of funds by opportunistic solicitor Vholes, he is convinced he'll be rich when the Jarndyce case is settled and haunts the courts even when his health is failing, but Woodcourt remains a faithful friend. The news that the case is settled – with all the assets gone in legal costs and no money left – kills him. His wife Ada is left expecting their child: a boy, named Richard Carstone.

CHADBAND, MRS (XIX), "stern, severe-looking", is the onetime maidservant of Lady Dedlock's long-forgotten sister – who took charge of a baby given up for dead. The sister "sternly nurtured" the child for the first years of her life. Now Mrs

Chadband, nearly 20 years later and married to verbose preacher Chadband, gives the inquisitive law clerk Guppy the background to Esther's early years.

DEDLOCK, SIR LEICESTER, BART. (II), proud and arrogant landowner of the Chesney Wold estate in Lincolnshire, in his late sixties, "family as old as the hills", honourable, obstinate and "intensely prejudiced".

When Mrs Rouncewell's elder son, the ironmaster, comes to ask that Lady Dedlock's maid Rosa be permitted to leave and improve her education before marrying the ironmaster's son, the baronet regards this as an affront to his dignity and sends him away.

Sir Leicester offers a hundred guineas reward for the apprehension of the murderer of the lawyer Tulkinghorn and tells Inspector Bucket he will meet every expense to avenge this "diabolical occurrence". He registers shock when Bucket reveals his wife's affair, as confirmed by the stolen papers that a moneylender, Smallweed, comes forward to produce.

Bucket produces the real murderer, the maid Hortense. With humiliation complete and no secrets left, Sir Leicester has a stroke. Bucket is commissioned to find his wife, who is missing.

Finding her dead comes as a terrible blow; Trooper George Rouncewell is brought to see the ailing man, who welcomes him as "the young man who so often carried my spare gun at Chesney Wold". He tells George that the message should go out that he feels towards his wife just as he did before and that his "strongest affection" for her remains undiminished. The baronet's health declines; George keeps watch and helps him to ride his horse over the estate.

★★★DEDLOCK, LADY (HONORIA) (II), fine face, elegant figure, in her forties and therefore some 20 years younger than her husband. She is "at the top of the fashionable tree" and "has an air of superiority, of power, and fascination". The share she has in a longstanding lawsuit called Jarndyce and Jarndyce (i.e. expectation of wealth) is the only property she brought her husband on their marriage. The story opens when the Dedlocks' lawyer Tulkinghorn is reading to her and her husband from records in Chancery.

Weeks later, she receives from Tulkinghorn the copy of a document in the Jarndyce lawsuit and asks him where he got it as she seems to recognise the handwriting. Tulkinghorn reports it was produced by a freelance copyist who was found dead, adding that the man – doing such humdrum work for little pay – had apparently come down in the world.

She also reads in the newspapers of the inquest on the copyist. Tulkinghorn directs her to the boy who gave evidence: the crossing-sweeper Jo.

Heavily veiled, she goes to Jo incognito and asks him to show her every place concerned with the copyist, where he lived and where he was buried: she is appalled ("what a scene of horror!") at the derelict patch of soil deemed suitable for a burial.

The young law clerk Guppy comes to her and says he has discovered that Esther Summerson's true name is Esther Hawdon. Lady Dedlock maintains haughty silence. He adds that quite recently a mysterious woman came to see where a humble law-copyist is buried: he promsies to bring some legal papers the next day.

Lady Dedlock goes to her room and breaks down. She weeps over "my child, my child", which she was told had died at birth but who had been taken and "sternly nurtured" by her religious sister.

Guppy come to tell her that the papers he promised to trace for her have been destroyed with the death of shopkeeper Krook; Lady Dedlock seems to give a sigh of relief.

In Lincolnshire she happens to see Esther sitting alone, goes to her and confesses she is her mother. They tearfully embrace; Lady Dedlock tells she had never again encountered her stern older sister who took charge of the baby Esther.

Tulkinghorn informs the Dedlocks in broad terms of the mishaps of a woman of prominence but mentions no names. Lady

Dedlock goes to his office to say this means she must leave her husband as she can no longer go on. Tulkinghorn tells her that for the honour of the family it's essential she stays.

Weeks later she again decides she must go, transfers her maid Rosa to the protection of the ironmaster Rouncewell, and is warned by Tulkinghorn that she must not leave. The same evening an old moneylender, Smallweed, is haggling with Dedlock and Bucket about selling stolen letters, Guppy comes to Lady Dedlock and tells her the papers he thought lost have fallen into Smallweed's hands: so the revelation she feared most will happen and "her name will be in many mouths".

She writes her husband a note saying she is not guilty of the murder and apologising for everything else; she bids him adieu and leaves her home.

Sir Leicester commissions Bucket to help find his wife; Bucket enlists Esther to join him, and later Woodcourt. The inspector has his informants; they lead him to the stationer Snagsby, where they find a note saying: "It was right that all that had sustained me should give way at once and that I should die of terror and my conscience."

They find Lady Dedlock dead in the graveyard where her lover Hawdon is buried.

FLITE, MISS (V), eccentric woman who covers all the twists and turns of the Jarndyce case by coming into court daily. As a suitor she "expects a judgement shortly", she tells Esther. Her flat overlooks Lincoln's Inn, where she shows them her collection of linnets and other birds in cages which she has promised to set free when judgement is given.

Friendly young physician Dr Woodcourt is called in when Miss Flite is unwell. When Esther comes to visit it is the second time she has met him. Miss Flite whispers that he is the "kindest physician in the college".

When Esher is recovering from smallpox Miss Flite walks the 20 miles from London to Bleak House on foot to see her and tells her still hopeful: "I expect a judgment shortly. Then I shall release my birds – and confer estates." When the case is settled (with no money left), she opens the cages.

★★★**GUPPY, WILLIAM (IV)**, clerk in the Kenge and Carboy office. As he is known to the Dedlocks' lawyer Tulkinghorn and the Jarndyce case, he comes to Bleak House uncommonly smart in a "new suit of glossy clothes", makes it clear from the start he is much struck by Esther and when they are alone falls to his knees and proposes. She tells him: "Get up from that ridiculous position" and sends him away, laughing about it afterwards. But she is made unhappy when she comes to London and finds him stalking her every time she goes to the theatre.

Guppy comes to visit Lady Dedlock and tells her he has discovered Esther Summerson's real name is Esther Hawdon. Also, quite recently, a mysterious well-dressed woman came to a pauper's graveyard to see where an unknown law-copyist was buried. Guppy admits he wants to get to the bottom of this matter in the hope that it will make Esther accept him.

Further to this purpose, he goes to the slum dwelling of the old shopkeeper Krook to be handed some stolen letters apparently in a feminine hand found in the room where his mysterious tenant (i.e. Captain Hawdon) died. Krook fails to appear as arranged and on investigation Guppy finds only his room full of smoke, some burnt floorboards and white ash: Krook has perished by spontaneous combustion.

The letters are thought to be destroyed; Guppy goes immediately to Lady Dedlock to report this: she seems relieved.

On the night that Bucket arrests Hortense and the moneylender Smallweed haggles with Bucket and Sir Leicester about selling the papers (which have survived), Guppy comes to tell Lady Dedlock this.

When John Jarndyce has stood back in order to let Esther marry Allan Woodcourt, Mr Guppy arrives to announce that he is now out of his articles, setting up in business for himelf as an attorney and therefore renews his proposal of marriage to Miss Summerson. With some hilarity he is sent packing by Mr Jarndyce.

HORTENSE, MADEMOISELLE (XII), 32, Lady Dedlock's French maid, a large-eyed brown woman, tight of face, who "seems to go about like a very neat She-Wolf imperfectly tamed" and is described by a bystander as "powerful high and passionate".

After she is sacked by Lady Dedlock, Hortense comes to Esther and with great intensity offers to be her maid, an offer Esther cannot accept. The Frenchwoman leaves.

She next appears in the Dedlocks' drawing room, having been summoned by the detective Bucket during his review of the Tulkinghorn murder. He had put her off her guard by letting her hear him saying he was sure George had shot the lawyer. He tells of the evidence against her: she was seen on the stairs on the night of the killing, the pistol she used was recovered. She loudly protests as she is led away.

*** JARNDYCE, JOHN (VI), owner of Bleak House, a mansion near St Albans. He is a man of nearer 60 than 50, "upright, hearty and robust", with a handsome lively face and "a pleasant expression in his eyes".

Appointed Esther Summerson's guardian, he gives a warm welcome to Esther and the two cousins Richard Carstone and Ada Clare, who are living at Bleak House under the terms of a court order. He asks Esther to call him Guardian and appoints her the Bleak House housekeeper, keeping all the keys.

He explains that the Jarndyce lawsuit involves a will and "that the original merits of the case have long disappeared", so that the proceedings have become solely an issue of costs with no prospect of solution.

When he gets to know Esther's background, he proposes marriage in a gentle, fatherly way, saying that if she refuses the existing friendship can continue as before. Esther accepts.

She then has a marriage proposal from Woodcourt and rejects it because of her pledge and tells Jarndyce she is happy to marry him next month.

He calls her to travel to a place which he claims needs her housekeeping skills; she finds a pretty cottage with everything arranged as she herself would like it. Jarndyce then confesses he knows that she really loves Woodcourt although she would have married him (Jarndyce) from "a sense of duty and affection" but he will stand aside to let her marry the man she really loves. And he shows her that the cottage prepared for her and Woodcourt has a name on the porch: "Bleak House". Mr Guppy calls to renew his offer to marry Esther; Mr Jarndyce good-humouredly dismisses him.

The Court of Chancery announces a settlement; the case is closed because all the assets have been taken up by legal costs. Mr Jarndyce expresses relief.

JELLYBY, CAROLINE (CADDY) (IV), Mrs Jellyby's eldest daughter, an ink-stained, "jaded and unhealthy looking" teenager who acts as her secretary ("I'm always writing for Ma"). She is unhappy that she and her siblings are much neglected. Esther listens to her worries and wins her friendship.

As much to escape from her mother's domination as anything else, she gets engaged to Prince Turveydrop, a young dancing master. Esther and Ada are bridesmaids at the wedding.

JELLYBY, MRS (IV), "a pretty, very diminutive plump woman, of from 40 to 50 with handsome eyes", is the mother of a large family, which she neglects as she is concerned solely with her "African project", raising funds to families cultivating coffee and "educating the natives of Borrioboola-Gha" on the banks of the Niger. She is untidily dressed and runs the project in a dirty untidy room in her home in Thavies Inn near Holborn.

She pays little attention when her husband is declared bankrupt or when her daughter Caddy is married, but when the African project fails she turns her efforts to taking up "the right of women to sit in Parliament".

★★★**JO (XI)**, barefoot crossing-sweeper in Holborn, illiterate and living in a dirty tenement Tom-all-Alone's, gets friendly words from only one person, the legal copyist who did a job for Tulkinghorn and who is found dead in his garret from an opium overdose. At the inquest on this stranger, Jo cannot give the coroner any information about him but as a mark of respect comes at night to sweep clear the access to his pauper's grave and says: "He wos wery good to me, he wos."

A little later he has a visit from a heavily veiled woman, Lady Dedlock, who wants to see all the places connected with the copyist, including where he was buried.

Police inspector Bucket traces Jo and brings him to Tulkinghorn's chambers, where the lawyer has dressed the French maid Hortense in Lady Dedlock's clothes: Jo identifies the clothes but not the wearer: Tulkinghorn is satisfied the mystery woman was Lady Dedlock.

Jo gets to meet Esther and he comments on the striking likeness between her and "t'other one", i.e. Lady Dedlock. Esther is worried at the boy's feverish condition and wishes to have him nursed, but he flees, leaving her with the affliction she has caught from him, smallpox.

Allan Woodcourt, young doctor newly returned from the east, comes across Jo hollow-eyed, starving and emaciated. Jo tells him he fled from Bleak House after being threatened.

Woodcourt finds the boy safe shelter at George's shooting gallery. Snagsby comes and leaves some money and John Jarndyce comes to see him and weeps over him; as Jo lies dying he asks to be buried beside Captain Hawdon in the graveyard to which he took Lady Dedlock.

KENGE, MR (III), solicitor in the Lincoln's Inn firm of Kenge and Carboy, long involved in the lawsuit Jarndyce and Jarndyce, which he describes as one of the greatest Chancery suits known, with costs already climbing to £70,000.

He is a "loquacious gentleman" known generally as "Conversation Kenge". He fetches away the orphan Esther Summerson, first to her school and then to London to arrange for her job at Bleak House.

At the end of the story, Kenge accompanies Esther and Woodcourt to the Court of Chancery, where it is announced that the case of Jarndyce and Jarndyce is closed. He praises it as "a monument of Chancery practice".

KROOK, MR (V), eccentric shopkeeper with a hairy cap and a cat on his shoulder called Lady Jane. He lives in his rag and bone shop by the wall of Lincoln's Inn. Miss Flite, the old lady following all the twists in the Jarndyce lawsuit, lives on his top floor; another tenant is the law-copyist found dead from an opium overdose.

As the copyist lay dying, Krook purloined a bundle of letters from his portmanteau. A friend notifies Guppy, who comes to fetch the letters, which he is told are in a feminine hand. Krook is overdue for a meeting to hand them over.

Guppy and a friend go to his room and find it filled with "smouldering suffocating vapour", a burnt patch of flooring and some white ashes: Mr Krook has disappeared, a victim of spontaneous combustion.

ROUNCEWELL, MRS (VII), has for 50 years been housekeeper at Chesney Wold, Lincolnshire seat of Sir Leicester Dedlock. She is "a fine old lady, handsome, stately, wonderfully neat". She has two sons, one a successful ironmaster but "the younger ran wild and went for a soldier and never came back".

London lawyer's clerk Mr Guppy and a companion come to see the great house while the owners are away. Mrs Rouncewell permits them to look at the family portraits; Guppy is much struck by the painting of Lady Dedlock and says, "I know her" although he has never met her.

After being parted for many years, Mrs Rouncewell is brought reunited with her son George, in prison on a murder charge.

ROUNCEWELL, ironmaster (XXVIII), "a little over 50, of a good figure, like his mother"; a clear voice and a shrewd open face. He has a son who wants to marry Rosa, Lady Dedlock's maid.

He comes to Sir Leicester to ask if the girl can be taken away to be given before her marriage some education beyond the basics she had at the local village school. Dedlock takes this as an affront to his estate's amenities and refuses.

Rouncewell does well in the elections, trouncing Sir Leicester and his party. The baronet welcomes the fact that his wife will keep Rosa as her maid, thus keeping her from "contamination" with the upstarts.

Rouncewell calls again in the Dedlocks' London home when Lady Dedlock has decided to dismiss Rosa and takes her away with him. Rosa is to marry Rouncewell's son – and newly recovered brother George is to give the bride away.

ROUNCEWELL, GEORGE (XXI), swarthy brown man of 50, "wellmade and good-looking", generally known as Trooper George, is the ex-soldier son of Mrs Rouncewell. He says of himself he was a vagabond. He now owns the run-down "George's Shooting Gallery" near Haymarket. He gives Richard Carstone weapons training when the young man prepares to join the army.

Trooper George is called to Tulkinghorn's office and shown an affidavit in the Jarndyce case: the lawyer points out he knows George was a serjeant (*sic*) to an army officer called Hawdon and asks if George has a sample of Hawdon's handwriting to see if it matches. George stalls.

He gets into trouble with debt and when he sees Tulkinghorn again yields to pressure over the money and resentfully hands him the paper the lawyer wanted.

When Tulkinghorn is found dead Inspector Bucket, knowing George's feelings towards the lawyer, arrests him for murder. In his prison cell he is visited by Esther, accompanied by Woodcourt and John Jarndyce.

While he is still in his cell, a friend of George's reunites him with his mother. He is freed, is warmly welcomed when he makes contact with his wealthy brother and though invited to join his firm prefers to stay at Chesney Wold, acting as a loyal groom when Sir Leicester goes out riding.

SKIMPOLE, HAROLD (VI), persuasive and inadequate parasite under the protection of Mr Jarndyce and proud of being incapable of dealing with life's problems. Richard and Esther pay off a debt to keep him out of gaol, assistance he dismisses as an opportunity for them to "develop generosity". He exerts bad influence; he has the crossing-sweeper Jo thrown out on the street when suffering from smallpox; and he encourages Richard's false assumption that the Jarndyce case will be settled and make him rich.

SNAGSBY, MR (X), law-stationer of Cook's Court near Chancery Lane, is visited by lawyer Tulkinghorn who wants to know who copied a document in the Jarndyce case; Snagsby reveals he farmed out the job to be done by one of his freelances.

He takes the lawyer to a shop near Lincoln's Inn owned by the rag merchant Krook, who rents out rooms, one of them to the man who fulfilled this commission. Tulkinghorn goes up and in a dilapidated garret finds the man dead of an opium overdose.

★★★SUMMERSON, ESTHER (III), (*heroine of the story relates her experiences in the first person*). Born illegitimate and cared for in her early years by a loveless, zealously religious aunt, and later educated at a school for training governesses, Esther begins life by being "timid and retiring" but in her six years at the school her affectionate personality makes her universally liked. Throughout the story she is, as her eventual suitor Woodcourt puts it, always "inspired by sweet consideration for others, and so free from a selfish thought".

In her teens she leaves the school and is told she is to report to a Mr Jarndyce. Before she goes to meet him she is introduced to two people also going to him, Ada Clare and Richard Carstone, wards of court in the Jarndyce lawsuit. Esther is court-appointed companion to Ada.

Mr John Jarndyce, owner of the mansion Bleak House, immediately takes to Esther and makes her his housekeeper. She always carries all the keys of the house.

Mr Guppy, young clerk at the law firm of Kent and Carboy, visits Bleak House on business and proposes to Esther without success.

On a visit to Lincolnshire, Esther attends morning service in the Dedlocks' parish church and meets for the first time the "handsome proud eyes" of Lady Dedlock and she instinctively feels "I knew the beautiful face".

Esther's personality draws people to her. Carstone comes to her to confess he is now tired of the law and wishes to go into the army. Her friend Caddy Jellyby comes to her and pleads with her to give her strength by being present when she announces her engagement to Turveydrop to his father and her mother. She helps to arrange Caddy's wedding and is a bridesmaid.

She visits Miss Flite, who is attended by a friendly physician who is highly spoken of, Dr Allan Woodcourt. When the young doctor leaves Britain for a job as a ship's surgeon in the Far East, she meets him again and he leaves her a nosegay.

She takes in the ailing crossing-sweeper Jo, desperately ill, and wants to continue nursing him but he disappears after being threatened by Bucket and Skimpole.

Esther catches Jo's smallpox, is confined to her room for weeks and withdraws from company because her face is scarred.

She hears that Dr Woodcourt has acquitted himself bravely in rescuing people in a shipwreck in the East and reflects that she is glad he did not tell her (as she feels he might have done) that he loved her because "the poor face he had known as mine was quite gone from me".

Lady Dedlock sees Esther sitting in the open air on her own, comes to her, falls on her knees and says: "I am your wicked and unhappy mother. O try to forgive me!" They soon exchange confidences.

John Jarndyce is told. He proposes marriage to Esther but says if she refuses things can carry on as they were, i.e. she can remain his housekeeper. She accepts his proposal.

She goes to Kent to meet Richard Carstone who has once again made a mess of his career. She meets Dr Woodcourt just off a vessel from India and pleads with him to be a friend to Richard.

When Trooper George is arrested for Tulkinghorn's murder, Esther is called to visit him with Jarndyce and Woodcourt. George takes one look at Esther and says she is remarkably like the cloaked figure he saw on the stairs at the lawyer's chambers the night of the murder.

When news comes of Lady Dedlock's disappearance Esther is called in by Bucket to help find her. They discover a note saying she will die "of terror and my conscience", and find her dead in the graveyard where Hawdon lies.

Esther and Woodcourt for once finding themselves alone, Woodcourt declares his love. She says that she is already spoken for – and tells John Jarndyce she will marry him next month.

Jarndyce asks her to take a trip to a property where he says her housekeeping advice is needed. He leads her to a charming cottage where she finds everything as she would want it herself. Jarndyce then declares himself: he doesn't want Esther to marry him out of "duty and affection" and stands aside so she can marry Woodcourt. The cottage he is giving them to live in has a name on the porch: Bleak House.

When she is all set to marry Woodcourt, Mr Guppy calls to announce he is out of his articles, will set up in business on his own as an attorney and boldly proposes marriage to Esther again; John Jarndyce sends him away.

Esther and Woodcourt are married and hear in the Court of

Chancery that the case of Jarndyce and Jarndyce has been settled; nothing is left because of legal costs.

Esther and Woodcourt settle into the cottage given the name of the new Bleak House; they have two daughters. Mr Jarndyce often comes to stay. Her husband has a regular practice, she enjoys her standing as the doctor's wife and they are happy.

***TULKINGHORN, MR (II),** solicitor to the Dedlock family, an old-fashioned gentleman dressed always in sombre black, "the silent depository of … a mysterious halo of family confidences" and "used to making his cramped nest in holes and corners of human nature".

At the start of the story he is reading some new legal documents from the case of Jarndyce and Jarndyce, to which Lady Dedlock is in some way a party.

Some time later, Tulkinghorn is curious about the way a document in the Jarndyce lawsuit was copied, and asks his agent Snagsby to take him to this person. In a filthy second-floor room, Tulkinghorn and Snagsby find the copyist newly dead from an overdose of opium.

This man had done other copying work but no-one knew his name or background. An inquest is held and no information can be gained except from a crossing sweeper called Jo, who was said to be the only person who spoke to this stranger.

The man is buried and Tulkinghorn reports to Lady Dedlock about him and that he is dead; it was she who had asked who had produced this paper because she had recognised the handwriting.

Tulkinghorn hears that a mystery woman has been to town to visit a pauper's grave. The crossing-sweeper Jo who led the woman there is traced, and is brought to Tulkinghorn's chambers, where the lawyer has dressed the maid Hortense in Lady Dedlock's clothing. The boy identifies the clothes, but not the wearer: Tulkinghorn, never averse to doing some sleuthing on his own account when he sees a mystery somewhere, is satisfied Jo's visitor was Lady Dedlock.

Tulkinghorn asks the soldier Mr George, onetime sergeant to Captain Hawdon, for the sample of Hawdon's handwriting he is eager to acquire to further his hold on Lady Dedlock. George stalls, but when he gets into trouble with a debt he surrenders the paper to Tulkinghorn in return for the debt being waived.

Lady Dedlock comes to see the lawyer when he has sketched to Sir Leicester the broad outline of her history without mentioning names, and she tells him she must leave as she can no longer live with her husband. Tulkinghorn becomes stern: in the interests of Sir Leicester, of the estate, of the honour of the family she should stay put; for a time she yields to this pressure.

Hortense comes to him to say she has been misused; he dismisses her. One evening he comes home from again warning Lady Dedlock not to leave home and is found in his chambers the next morning, shot through the heart. A murder hunt follows.

TURVEYDROP, PRINCE (XIV), a "little blue-eyed fair young man" of 30 who runs a dancing school. He has small dancing shoes, a threadbare suit and a feminine manner. He has to support his vain widowed father. Prince marries Caddy Jellyby and takes her to Gravesend for a week's honeymoon.

VHOLES, MR (XXXII), "a sallow man with pinched lips, face tall and thin aged about 50, a black, buttoned-up unwholesome figure", including sable gloves, has been engaged by Richard Carstone in the Jarndyce case and lures Richard to a court hearing in London although he admits to Esther that there will be no useful outcome. He tells Richard he keeps the case alive on his behalf – to no purpose – and drains him of funds until the young man dies.

★★★WOODCOURT, DR ALLAN (XIII), a "dark young surgeon" to whom Esther is introduced at a dinner party: "he was rather reserved, but I thought him very sensible and agreeable". She meets him again when he is attending Miss Flite.

Having practised for four years without financial success, he comes to take leave of Esther and Ada before going abroad as a ship's surgeon. As he departs he kisses Esther's hand and leaves a nosegay.

Months later Esther hears from Miss Flite that Allan was involved in a shipwreck in the Far East and took charge of the victims and generally conducted himself so much a "calm and brave" hero that the survivors knelt at his feet.

Esther goes to Deal to lend support to Carstone, who is giving up yet another career, the army this time. While there she meets Woodcourt, who has come back from the Far East, his financial situation no better than before. As he plans to go to London Esther urges him to be a friend and support to the vacillating Carstone.

Woodcourt meets crossing-sweeper Jo, who is in the last stages of smallpox. He arranges for Jo to have shelter and food at George's shooting gallery and give him medical aid until the boy dies.

Woodcourt joins Esther and Inspector Bucket in the final hunt for Lady Dedlock, whom they find dead in the graveyard where the father of her child was buried.

With Richard Carstone in trouble after failing in yet another career, Woodcourt acts as a protector, though he cannot prevent Richard haunting the court daily in the hope of a settlement. He remains a loyal supporter to the end.

Woodcourt and Esther find themselves alone; he declares his love. She tells him she is not free.

John Jarndyce stands back to allow Esther to marry Woodcourt. All is settled when Guppy calls to renew his offer of marriage to Esther and is sent away.

Woodcourt attends the Court of Chancery and hears the judgment that the case is closed, with all assets swallowed in legal costs. He comforts his friend Carstone, for whom the news is too much in his failing health.

He and Esther live in the cottage called the new Bleak House, and have two daughters.

DAVID COPPERFIELD

Sent to work in a London warehouse at the age of 10, this is how David sees himself: "It is a matter of some surprise to me, even now, that I can have been so easily thrown away at such an age. A child of excellent abilities and with strong powers of observation, quick, eager, delicate, and soon hurt bodily or mentally, it seems wonderful to me that nobody should have made any sign on my behalf. But none was made..."

BARKIS (V), good-humoured local carrier who takes the young David to Yarmouth on the boy's way to school in London. He hears how Peggotty is good at baking and cooking and asks David to give her a message, *"Barkis is willin'"*, which David promises to pass on. When he comes back for the holidays, Barkis transports him again and says he is still waiting for an answer. David relays the message and Peggotty says laughing that what Barkis wants is to marry her.

He does – and turns out to be careful with money, doling it out from his strongbox, which when he dies is found to hold more than £3,000. David, now aged about 20, is with him as he is dying: his last words are once again *"Barkis is willin'"*.

COPPERFIELD, CLARA (I), David's mother. Pretty and gentle, she was a diffident governess when she marred David's father, also called David, who died early and left her £150 a year. Her constant companion is the faithful maidservant Peggotty.

When the suitor Murdstone makes his appearance both Peggotty and the boy draw away from him. Murdstone marries Clara and soon moulds her pliant character as he wishes and brings in his sister

Jane. Between the two all household decisions are taken out of the hands of Clara, who is all the more unhappy when David is banished to school.

David comes back after his half-term and finds he has a half-brother; and that his mother is more crushed than ever. Just after he goes back to school she dies; the baby dies a day later.

★★★**COPPERFIELD, DAVID (I)**, eponymous hero, is born in Blunderstone, Suffolk, on a Friday midnight in March to Mrs Clara Copperfield, whose husband, also called David, had died six months previously. Widow and son live together happily with the family servant, Peggotty.

When he is eight David is introduced to Edward Murdstone, his mother's suitor, and draws away from him. David is taken for a blissful holiday in Yarmouth with Peggotty's family and when he comes back his mother and Murdstone are married. He is unhappy, finding refuge only in his books. Murdstone tells David that he expects obedience, and he and his sister make the hitherto cheerful, happy boy "sullen, dull and dogged".

Murdstone manhandles David and the boy retaliates, biting his hand hard. For this he is caned, imprisoned in his room and banished to school in London.

At the harsh Salem House school, he suffers beatings from brutal headmaster Creakle, but wins the friendship and protection of senior pupil Steerforth. He goes home for the holidays and finds his mother with a baby – neither robust. Both die shortly afterwards.

David is left with the Murdstones. They do not want him, so at the age of 10 he is farmed out to the Blackfriars warehouse/wine firm of Murdstone and Grinby as a "miserable labouring hind" at a salary of 6s. a week. He finds a room in City Road with a family called Micawber.

When the Micawbers leave he decides to quit his job and look up his aunt Betsey Trotwood in Kent; on the way he is robbed and arrives at her cottage in Dover destitute and starving. She shelters him and becomes his guardian; when the Murdstones come to fetch him back she sends them away.

David is sent to Dr Strong's school in Canterbury, where he is happy. He boards with hard-drinking lawyer Wickfield and is charmed by his daughter Agnes, a girl of his own age with a "quiet good calm spirit", which deeply impresses him. He also meets the lawyer's articled clerk, Uriah Heep, always professing he is "umble". He stays at the school long enough to become head boy, leaves at age 17.

Aunt Trotwood pays a premium of £1,000 to article him to the law firm of Spenlow and Jorkins in the Doctors' Commons by St Paul's Cathedral.

Invited to visit his employer, Mr Spenlow, he meets his gentle teenage daughter Dora and falls in love. They become secretly engaged. He takes a part-time additional job to earn another £70 a year and explains to Dora that he has to because he is poor.

Dora's reaction is "Please don't be practical. Because it frightens me so." David is "charmed by her childish winning way".

Spenlow dies and Dora goes to live with two elderly aunts, who treat her like a child. When David tells Dora she is entitled to be treated rationally, Dora says they are kind to her and bursts into tears. The aunts permit his courtship.

At age 21, David is an established shorthand writer in Parliament and becomes a freelance journalist and then an author.

David and Dora are married and set up house, chaotically. If he asks his wife to be practical she retorts that that is worse than a scolding, and weeps. She calls herself his child-wife and he writes: "I was a boyish husband as to years."

Dora is a devoted wife who cannot cope. Her heath begins to fail; slowly she fades and after she calls on Agnes to be with her she dies.

Some years pass. David becomes an established author, keeps in contact with Agnes and eventually realises his feelings for her go beyond "respect and honour". They talk it over; she admits "I have loved you all my life" and adds that when dying Dora urged her "to occupy this vacant place".

David and Agnes are married. They are happy and have children.

HEEP, URIAH (XV), articled clerk to the lawyer Mr Wickfield with whom David boards in Canterbury. Red-haired red-eyed young man with skeletal fingers, habitually rubbing his hands together, dressed in black, constantly refers to himself as being the "umblest person going": Uriah "had a way of writhing when he wanted to express enthusiasm, which was very ugly".

Years pass. Heep engages Micawber as his confidential clerk. Gradually assuming total ascendancy in the Wickfield household, he makes a play for Agnes's hand – which fails.

Micawber sets up a meeting in Heep's own office: with David and Betsey present he unmasks Heep as guilty of theft, fraud and embezzlement, and compels him to return all his booty. David finds Heep in prison reading a hymnbook and professing bogus penitence.

"LITTLE EM'LY" (III), Peggotty's orphaned niece, becomes David's playmate on his first visit to the Peggotty family in Great Yarmouth; becomes engaged to her cousin Ham Peggotty; runs away with her seducer Steerforth; her letter says: "I will be never come back unless he brings me back a lady."

In Naples Steerforth tires of her, tries to marry her off to his manservant Littimer; she flees and eventually makes her way back to England. Ham is drowned; she and her uncle Dan'el emigrate to Australia, where she becomes "quiet and timid", helping others.

★★★MICAWBER, WILKINS (XI), middle-aged, stout, bald and with an eye-glass and "a genteel manner", married to uncritical wife Emma with four children, has lodgings in City Road. David Copperfield has a room there when he starts his work at the Blackfriars firm. Mr Micawber is constantly beset by creditors: he advises David: *'Annual income twenty pounds, annual expenditure nineteen, nineteen six, result happiness. Annual income twenty pounds, annual expenditure twenty pounds ought and six, result misery.'*

When David is a pupil in Canterbury he meets Mr Micawber as genial as ever, still waiting "for something to turn up". It doesn't and the Micawbers leave for London, their hotel bill unpaid.

When they meet again in London Mrs Micawber is expecting their fifth child and her husband, plausible as ever, burdens David's vulnerable old school friend Tommy Traddles with a debt.

The family moves back to Canterbury when Heep engages Micawber as confidential clerk.

Time passes. Micawber amasses enough evidence to call in David and others and unmask Uriah, calling him "you Heep of infamy" and compelling him to return all the assets of the Wickfield firm.

Betsey Trotwood pays for the Micawber family to accompany Mr Peggotty and Em'ly to Australia, where, as Mr Micawber puts it, "something of an extraordinary nature will turn up on that shore".

After 10 years news comes that he has become a "diligent and esteemed" local journalist and magistrate, all debts settled.

***MURDSTONE, EDWARD (II)**, with black hair, whiskers and ill-omened black eyes, pays court to widowed Mrs Copperfield. After the marriage he dominates both mother and son, assisted by his sister Jane. When he manhandles David the boy bites his hand; soon afterwards David is banished to Salem House school in London.

Murdstone weeps at his wife's death, but neglects his stepson and gets rid of him in a London warehouse. When Miss Trotwood writes to him after David has fled to her cottage in Dover, he and his sister go there to take him back and are sent packing.

MURDSTONE, JANE (IV), elder sister of Edward, dark, "heavy eyebrows nearly meeting over her large nose", moves in after her brother's marriage, she is harsh to both David and his mother.

***PEGGOTTY, CLARA (I)**, Mrs Copperfield's loyal maidservant always known only by her surname. When Mr Murdstone comes a-courting, Peggotty warns Mrs Copperfield against him, much to the latter's distress.

She takes David on a holiday to her Yarmouth home, a converted boat on the seashore wth a funnel for a chimcy. Head of the family there is her fisherman brother Dan'el Peggotty, who lives with his jovial nephew Ham and a niece, "Little Em'ly".

Peggotty laughs off the message *"Barkis is willin'"* from the local carrier but when she is sacked after David's mother dies she goes back to Yarmouth and marries him. Over the years she and David keep in contact. In late middle age she becomes housekeeper to Betsey Trotwood.

PEGGOTTY, DAN'EL (III), fisherman brother of David's old nurse, "deals in lobsters, crabs and crawfish". When he hears his niece has eloped with Steerforth, he goes to London and asks Mrs Steerforth to remedy matters by getting her son to marry the girl. She replies that that would ruin her son's career.

Mr Peggotty departs, determined to seek his niece. When she returns to England, they are reunited and emigrate to Australia.

***SPENLOW, DORA (XXVI)**, daughter of David's employer, is so "captivating, girlish, bright-eyed" that David falls in love with her when he visits the Spenlow home. She is diminutive, with "the gayest little laugh".

David and Dora become engaged. When he tells her he has had to take an extra part-time job to make some money, she replies: "Don't talk about being poor and working hard!… And Jip (her dog) must have a mutton chop every day at twelve or he'll die." Her friend Miss Mills speaks of her as "a favourite child of nature".

Dora's father discovers the affair, dismisses it as "youthful folly" and forbids the two to meet. The same night he collapses and dies; Dora is sent to stay in Putney with two spinster aunts, who permit the courtship. He marries Dora; before and after the wedding appeals to her to be practical fall on deaf ears: she calls herself his "child-wife".

David, a patient husband, makes sporadic efforts to make the household efficient, but to no avail, the more as Dora's health begins to fail.

Slowly she fades away. She calls on Agnes, who comes and stays until Dora dies.

***STEERFORTH, JAMES (VII)**, senior pupil aged about 15, good-looking, urbane and self-confident, takes David under his wing and greatly eases his time at Salem House school. When they meet again Steerforth, now at Oxford, has no aim in life. Agnes Wickfield warns David that he is "a dangerous friend". Shortly afterwards David hears of Steerforth's flight with Em'ly.

Steerforth's manservant Littimer, described by David as a scoundrel (who ends up in jail), informs Davd some time later that in Naples Steerforth abandoned Em'ly, suggesting as he departed that Littimer should marry Em'ly; the girl protested violently – and also vanished.

In a storm on the east coast of England Steerforth drowns in his yacht; David has to break the news to his mother. He goes to the room where his friend's body lies and "lifted up the leaden hand and held it to my heart".

***TROTWOOD, BETSEY (I)**, David's great-aunt, "a formidable personage" and "principal magnate of our family", lives in a cottage in a seaside village. She arrives before Mrs Copperfield's confinement firmly expecting a girl; when she is told that it's a boy she walks out.

Ten years later David flees London, and having been robbed on the way arrives at her cottage in Dover penniless and starving.

Miss Trotwood is "tall, hard-featured, but by no means ill-looking", with grey hair and "a very quick, bright eye", but becomes sturdily protective of David. When Murdstone and his sister come to fetch the boy away, Miss Trotwood accuses them of breaking David's mother "like a poor caged bird" and systematically mistreating her son; she takes over as David's guardian.

To start his new life, she advises him: "never be mean, never be false, never be cruel". She sends him to school in Canterbury but he regularly visits her in Dover. On leaving school she has him articled to a law firm in the Doctors' Commons.

She loses her fortune and comes to live with David in London; with the unmasking of Heep she gets her money back and returns to her Dover cottage.

***WICKFIELD, AGNES (XV)**, daughter of lawyer Wickfield with whom David boards in Canterbury. She is her widowed father's "little housekeeper", a girl of about David's age, with "a bright and happy face", and "a quiet good calm spirit ... that I never shall forget".

When David begins his articles in London he meets Agnes again and she warns him that Steerforth is bad company. She also says she is worried that Heep has achieved such an ascendancy over her father.

David comes to tell her about his blighted affair with Dora, and Agnes counsels him calmly and calls him "by the name of Brother". While David is there, Heep, now in control of the firm, makes a move to seek to marry her but is furiously repulsed by her father.

When Heep is disgraced, Agnes is restored to her assets; David calls her in as his wife's health is fading, and she is a source of comfort as Dora dies. Eventually he realises the depth of his love and marries Agnes. The book ends with a happy home and children.

DOMBEY AND SON

BAGSTOCK, JOSEPH (VII), "wooden-featured blue-faced Major with his eyes starting out of his head", a big stomach and a blustering manner. He usually refers to himself in the third person: "Joey Bagstock, Sir, he's hard-hearted and de-vilish sly!"

In Brighton he becomes a confidant to the tycoon Dombey and takes him to visit Leamington, where they meet Mrs Edith Granger and her mother Mrs Skewton. The Major praises the virtues of Dombey and Edith to each other to help promote the marriage.

BROWN, MRS (VI), a tramp who calls herself "Good Mrs Brown", is a "very ugly old woman with red rims around her eyes and a mouth that mumbled". She sees Florence Dombey in the street left unattended for a moment, seizes her, takes her home, makes her take off all her good clothes and puts her in rags before freeing her.

"Good Mrs Brown" reappears in the story much later, accompanied by her daughter Alice, a tall stately woman who has returned to Britain after having been a transported convict. On a begging trip Alice is given as an act of kindness some money by Harriet Carker, who lives with John Carker the Junior.

She learns who Harriet is and returns to the Carker cottage with her mother and throws back the money she has received, saying she could not accept it from "you whose name I spit upon".

James Carker is riding home one evening when he is watched by two people: Mrs Brown and her daughter. The mother says that she should get money from this man, Alice reminds her that she earlier rejected money from Harriet and that from this man here she would not touch a penny "unless I could poison it and send it back to him".

After the Dombey marriage break-up and Florence's departure, Mrs Brown meets Dombey in the street and tells him she knows where his wife and Carker have gone. He comes to her home and, hiding behind a door, hears a boy called Rob Toodle, employed by James Carker as a spy, reveal that Edith travelled alone and was to meet Carker in Dijon. Alice tells Dombey: "I have as good cause for my anger as you have for yours, and its object is the same man."

It comes out that Carker was once her husband. The marriage did not last long as he treated her badly, hence her reaction to Harriet.

Alice is on her death-bed; the forgiving Harriet goes to see her. The mother tells her the family's story: many years ago, two brothers, both men-about-town, married: one had a daughter Alice, the other had a daughter Edith: the two girls were therefore first cousins.

★★★**CARKER, JAMES (XIII)**, generally known as Mr Carker the Manager, "oily of tongue, cruel of heart", is Dombey's chief executive officer, aged 38 or 40, with a florid complexion and two unbroken rows of glistening teeth. In his manner to his employer he considered "there was no show of subservience … that I should think sufficient". By contrast, he bullies his brother and all subordinates.

Carker runs the firm very assiduously when his boss goes to Leamington and after some time goes there to report how business is doing. He meets Edith and her mother, and not only sizes up the situation immediately but also establishes a bond with Edith; both know that she is being sold like merchandise.

Some time after, he reminds her that he is aware of her affection for Florence and that if her husband were to be told Florence might well be sent away.

Dombey meets Carker and says that he is dissatisfied with his wife's conduct: "I informed Mrs Dombey that if I should find it necessary to object or remonstrate again, I should express my opinion through yourself, my confidential agent". Carker goes to Edith and again warns her: "I entreat you … to be cautious in your demonstrations of affection for Miss Dombey". Otherwise, "your continued show of affection will not benefit its object".

Carker is present when husband and wife have an open quarrel during their wedding anniversary dinner. He tries to make peace, for which he is upbraided by his employer.

Edith goes missing; Carker has eloped with her. He goes to meet her at the appointed rendezvous in Dijon, greeting her as his "charming wife".

She "shrunk and shivered" at his approach. Proud, imperious and hostile, after he speaks fondly of a future in Sicily, she tells him that "I struck a blow that laid your master in the dust", but "how many times has your bold knavery assailed me with outrage and insult?" He had been a "loathsome creature" to her and so "we meet and part tonight".

There is a knock. Edith withdraws; Carker escapes by a back door. He finds transport, gets to the coast and arrives back in England. He selects a quiet country area for safety but still but feels pursued.

He walks by the railway line early one morning as the sun is coming up and sees Dombey emerging at the little station. He flees, a train approaches at speed and he is crushed beneath its wheels.

CARKER, JOHN (XIII), is generally known in the Dombey office as Mr Carker the Junior, though he is two or three years older than his brother and is "quite resigned to occupy that low condition" because some years ago he stole money, a lever his brother uses to keep him down.

He lives quietly with his sister Harriet, who gives the wandering tramp Alice money out of kindness of heart; some hours later Alice and her mother return and the money is scornfully thrown back.

When James elopes with Edith, Dombey sacks John Carker.

With James's death all his assets come to Harriet and John, who decide that part of what they have inherited should secretly be passed to the bankrupt Dombey to help out.

CHICK, MRS LOUISA (I), Mr Dombey's sister, a busybody "rather past the middle age". In the weeks after her brother is widowed she steers the spinster Miss Tox in his direction; when after Dombey's Leamington visit Mrs Chick come to tell her that her brother is remarrying, Miss Tox faints and is roundly condemned for harbouring false hopes.

When Dombey is deserted by his wife, Louisa's expansive commiseration becomes burdensome to her brother.

CUTTLE, CAPTAIN NED (IV), "a very salt-looking man indeed", with a hook instead of right hand, is a regular Sunday visitor to his friend Sol Gills the instrument-maker.

Gills goes missing after Walter Gay's ship has apparently gone down and the Captain moves into the instrument-maker's shop. When Florence runs away from the family home and comes to stay with him he cares for her lovingly.

Walter comes back, having survived shipwreck, and meets his old love. The captain happily attends the quiet wedding of Walter and Florence. With the couple settled down in married life, Captain Cuttle goes into partnership with the safely returned Sol Gills and helps to revive the instrument-maker's business.

DOMBEY, EDITH, *see Granger, Edith*

★★★DOMBEY, FLORENCE (I), Mr Dombey's daughter, six years old when the story begins. A timid girl whose existence means nothing to her father; he keeps her at a distance so she, "so gentle, so quiet and so uncomplaining", is starved of affection. She is deeply attached to her sickly brother Paul. Charged with looking after her is a womanly black-eyed girl of 14, Susan Nipper.

While on an outing in central London, Florence is left alone in the street for a moment and kidnapped by an elderly thief calling herself "Good Mrs Brown", who takes her to her slum home and strips of her clothing, giving her rags in exchange. Florence is abandoned, wanders desolate in the City and is rescued by Walter Gay.

Florence and her brother are sent to Brighton for the sea air. When little Paul is enrolled in Blimber's boarding school, Florence, allowed to visit him at weekends, helps him with his schoolwork.

Florence, now 13, is with her brother when he dies. A week after the funeral she gets a visit from onetime Blimber head boy Toots, who makes her a present of the dog Diogenes, which Paul befriended at the school. She tries to forge a new bond with her father without success.

Florence goes to see Walter at Sol Gills's home before the young man leaves for the West Indies. She promises to keep in touch with the old instrument-maker and call him "Walter's Uncle". She bursts into tears when she tells Walter that, with little Paul dead, "I'll be your sister all my life and think of you like one wherever we may be".

Her father comes back from Leamington with Edith Granger and tells Florence coolly that she will be her new Mama. Florence impetuously embraces her; Edith says, "Begin by believing that I will try to make you happy"; Edith sees in the warm-hearted girl the person she could have been herself had she not been manipulated by her ambituous mother.

From then on Edith and Florence are close friends; Edith comes to Florence's room the night before the wedding, kisses her softly, weeps – and spends the night by her side.

Susan Nipper, servant and friend to Florence after 12 years, goes to Mr Dombey and pleads for her: "I've seen her … grow up to be a lady … that is the grace and pride of every company she goes in … and I've always seen her cruelly neglected … you don't know your own daughter, Sir, you don't know what you're doing … it's a sinful shame." Dombey is enraged and sacks her on the spot.

At 17, Florence is a woman of "modest self-reliance and deep intensity of feeling", with "a pensive air upon her beauty". She watches with dismay the growing chasm between her father and stepmother. She is present when at the dinner for their second wedding anniveriary husband and wife row openly; Florence leaves the room in tears. She meets Edith on the stairs, who tells her to "get way from me. Don't touch me!"

The next day Edith has vanished. When it comes out that she has eloped with Carker, Florence goes to her father intending to comfort him, but he knocks her to the ground: distressed, and bearing the mark of his blow on her body, "she realised she had no father upon earth and ran out, orphaned, from his house".

She finds refuge in the instrument-maker's shop; Captain Cuttle takes loving care of her; she settles down. A few days later Walter comes back, having survived shipwreck. The young couple are joyously reunited; as they plan their wedding Sol Gills suddenly walks in – he had been searching for his nephew in the West Indies and had come home as soon as he heard that the young man had survived.

Florence walks to the church with Walter for the ceremony; also present are Susan Nipper, Mr Toots, Sol Gills and Captain Cuttle.

Walter has a new job: he and his bride leave for Gravesend to take ship for China. When they come back to England they have a son, Paul.

Florence returns to the old house and finds her father alone, haggard and worn. They weep as each asks for forgiveness from the other.

Her father goes to live with the Gay family. In attendance on Florence is the faithful servant she had for so many years, Susan Nipper, now married to Mr Toots.

Aristocratic cousin Feenix comes to fetch Florence to a meeting in London: in the old house she meets Edith, her face "beautiful and stately yet". Edith asks if "the stain upon your name … will that ever be forgiven?" Florence replies: "Freely, freely, both by Walter and by me".

In the autumn, by the seashore, Florence has her white-haired father with her and her two children, Paul and a daughter – the old man's special favourite: "Little Florence, little Florence!" The faithful old dog Diogenes is also there.

★★★**DOMBEY, PAUL (I)**, head of the old-established wholesale and retail firm of Dombey and Son, aged about 48, rather bald and "though a handsome man, too stern and pompous … to be prepossessing". That his wife is dying after the birth of their child means nothing; in his "starched impenetrable dignity" the new baby is his obsession so that the firm can once again really be "Dombey and Son.".

The little boy, Paul, grows up weak and ailing. When Walter Gay calls for help because his uncle has financial difficulties, Dombey gets Paul, now six, to tell Walter he will be helped, the aim being to give his son an early lesson about the power of money.

After little Paul's death Florence goes up to her father's room to give him her devotion and is rudely repulsed. She leaves, crushed, while he remains behind and weeps for his lost boy.

Dombey becomes friends with Major Bagstock and travels with him to Leamington, where they meet Mrs Skewton and her handsome daughter Mrs Edith Granger.

The four people meet regularly and Dombey is drawn to Edith's proud and detached attitude. He proposes and is accepted; neither he nor Edith's mother notices her lack of emotional attraction, on her side because she knows she is being sold by her ambitious mother, on his side because he, too, has stifled emotion all his life.

Some time after the honeymoon and the couple have settled into their London mansion, Dombey goes up to Edith's room and says he is dissatisfied with her behaviour and demands her submission; she refuses. He engages his CEO, James Carker, to tell her to behave as he would wish; Carker is overjoyed at this increase in his hold over both of them.

On their second wedding anniversary, with Carker and Florence present, Dombey tells his wife to prepare for a social occasion to take place the next day. She refuses; they both dig in their heels and tempers rise. Edith says she wants a separation. Dombey is outraged at this possible affront to his dignity: "common people to talk of Mr Dombey and his domestic affairs!" Edith throws her diamond tiara on the floor and storms out. He retires to his room.

Edith is missing the next day. A coachman reveals that she was seen departing with Carker. Florence goes up to her father's room to comfort him but "he lifted up his cruel arm and struck her". She falls to the ground and runs out of the house.

He meets the beggar "Good Mrs Brown" in the street and she tells him she has information: he comes to her home and overhears Carker's own onetime spy, a boy named Rob Toodle, say that the fleeing couple are to meet at Dijon.

Dombey pursues them there and narrowly misses catching Carker. The chase continues; in the small country town where the quarry has sought refuge, Dombey arrives at the railway station just in time to see Carker fall under the wheels of an oncoming train.

The head of the firm resumes his business activities but "it is impossible to convince him, impossible to reason with him" that Dombey and Son is in serial decline. The outcome is bankruptcy.

Dombey himself remains in the house while his goods and furniture are sold and carted away. He sticks to his room, brooding and remorseful; when he looks into the mirror he sees "a spectral, haggard wasted likeness of himself".

He hears a well-known step approaching him. It is Florence, back in England. They fall into each other's arms, each asking forgiveness of the other.

He becomes gravely ill but gradually recovers and goes to live with Walter and Florence Gay. With nothing left of his own estate, he mysteriously gets "a certain annual sum" to live on, but he never gets to know it is through the generosity of John Carker the Junior and his sister Harriet.

In his eventide years he is "a white-haired gentleman whose face bears heavy marks of care and suffering," but he has pulled through and his only pride is in his daughter and her husband.

In the autumn they go walking along the beach, the white-haired gentleman, a young lady and two children, a boy and a girl – and the dog Diogenes.

DOMBEY, PAUL (I), newborn son on whom his father builds extravagant hopes. His mother dies some hours after his birth.

He grows up "wan and wistful", tires quickly and has "an old, old face". When he is five, still weak, he is taken to live in Brighton to benefit from the air; in his little carriage he is taken to the edge of the sea and asks Florence "what the waves are always saying".

At six years of age he is enrolled for what his father hopes will be "a vigorous course of education". The Brighton establishment is chosen: "Doctor Blimber's establishment was a great hothouse, in which there was a forcing apparatus incessantly at work … every description of Greek and Latin vegetable was got off the driest twigs of boys … nature was of no consequence at all."

In this atmosphere the boy is unhappy. His spirit begins to fade, he gets dizzy spells, the Apothecary diagnoses "want of vital power"; he is excused lessons. He wins general affection by making friends with everyone including the despised mongrel pet Diogenes. When he comes home at the end of term his father is distressed. On his last day he gets to see Walter and his father; Florence is with him when he dies.

★★★GAY, WALTER (IV), "fresh-faced, bright-eyed, curly-haired" boy of 14 newly taken on by the firm of Dombey and Son; nephew of instrument-maker Sol Gills, with whom he lives. Walter meets Florence Dombey in the street after a thief has waylaid her and stripped of her clothing, and returns her to her home. From that moment he is in love with her and thinks of her constantly.

Some years later, his uncle is in debt and Walter goes to Brighton to speak to his employer; the debt is paid and Sol's home is saved.

A vacancy occurs in the firm's counting-house in Barbados; because Walter once inadvertently talked to him of Florence, all mention of whom upsets him, her vindictive father decides on a whim that Walter should be sent away to the West Indies. Before he leaves Florence visits him and tells him that with little Paul dead she will always look on Walter as her brother.

Walter leaves for the West Indies in a ship called the *Son and Heir*; there is no news for so long that there are fears she may have foundered.

Months pass. Florence has fled her father's house after he assaulted her and gone to Captain Cuttle's in the instrument-maker's shop.

Walter returns: he survived the wreck of the *Son and Heir*. He is happily reunited with Florence. As they are planning to get married, they welcome the reappearance of Sol Gills, who had gone to the West Indies to trace his nephew and had come back as soon as he heard that Walter was safe.

On their wedding day Walter and Florence walk to the church for the ceremony. Also there are Susan Nipper, Mr Toots, Sol Gills and Captain Cuttle.

Walter has another job: the happy couple sail from Gravesend for China. When they return they have a son named Paul.

GILLS, SOLOMON (IV), kindly ships' instrument-maker, "slow, quiet-spoken", has a shop near East India House selling chronometers, telescopes and other navigational instruments; by the shop is a wooden effigy of a dapper midshipman with a telescope to his eye.

He regularly entertains his old friend and sea-dog Captain Cuttle. When there is, for a long time, no news of the ship in which Walter sailed for the West Indies, Sol Gills goes missing from his shop and the old Captain moves in to mind it.

Just before the wedding of Walter and Florence, quite unexpectedly Sol Gills comes back. He went to Barbados to seek his nephew, stayed there until he heard that Walter *had* been rescued, and took passage for England. There had been no news of him because letters he sent home had been misdirected.

With Walter out of the little midshipman's shop he decides to go into partnership with Captain Cuttle; as a result, the instrument-maker's business flourishes.

***GRANGER, MRS EDITH (XXI)** (afterwards Edith Dombey), "very handsome, very haughty, very wilful", still in her twenties and with a languid manner. Her mother is the vain ambitious Hon. Mrs Skewton. Before the story began Edith had already lost her army colonel husband and a child of the marriage.

Bagstock and Dombey meet her and her mother on their visit to Leamington and the Major tells Dombey that she is proud but of "high quality".

James Carker comes to Leamington to report to his boss and the manager spots Edith sitting by herself plainly wrestling with her situation; she is being steered into a marriage to a rich man she does not love. Without anything being said, he and Edith both see the reality.

She talks to her mother of a "sordid and miserable transaction: (Dombey) sees me at the auction, and he thinks it well to buy me". Carker "already knows us thoroughly and reads us right ... and before him I have even less self-respect".

Edith and Dombey come to his London house and when Florence comes in her father says coldly, "This lady will soon become your Mama" and his daughter spontaneously falls weeping on Edith's bosom. Edith says: "Begin by thinking well of me ... by believing that I will try to make you happy and that I am prepared to love you, Florence".

On the night before her wedding Edith comes to Florence's bed, kisses her softly, weeps – and spends the night by Florence's side.

She comes back from the Paris honeymoon and immediately picks up again the bond with Florence ("I will be your true friend always"); as for her husband, she remains "arrayed with all her soul against him". When he demands that she should obey all his wishes she refuses. He removes her, Mrs Skewton and Florence to Brighton. Mrs Skewton has a second stroke there, dies and is buried in Brighton.

When the wife comes back, the husband moves into a separate room. Edith feels emotionally isolated except for her loving link with Florence.

The couple drift apart. On the second anniversary of their wedding, with Carker and Florence present at dinner, Dombey tells his wife to prepare for another dinner the next day. She refuses. Both parties dig in and tempers rise. Edith says she wants a separation, which Dombey won't contemplate. She smashes her tiara, leaves the room and afterwards withdraws from talking to Florence.

She disappears and her husband finds all the jewels and fine clothing he has bought her piled up in her bedroom.

Edith travels alone to Southampton to take ship for France and meets Carker as arranged in Dijon. He expects a loving reunion; instead he is angrily told: "You have been a loathsome creature to me". Also, "I struck a blow that laid your lofty master in the dust". He tries to remonstrate, says they can be happy together in Sicily, but she tells him "We meet and part tonight."

There is a knocking, which shows the pair have been traced: Edith withdraws; Carker has a narrow escape through a back door.

Years later, Florence, now a wife and mother and living in the country, is escorted into London by Lord Feenix for an unexpected meeting: she finds herself with Edith, still stately and beautiful but passion and pride left their mark on her face.

Florence freely forgives her for the past and says her father will, too. She adds: "I can never forget that you were very good to me".

Edith calls her "my better angel" and adds that she was "guilty of a blind and passionate resentment" of which she will not repent, but also she was "not guilty with that dead man", i.e. she did not commit adultery.

Cousin Feenix tells Florence that he and Edith will retire to the south of Italy.

ROB THE GRINDER, *see TOODLE, ROBIN*

SKEWTON, THE HON. MRS (XXI), mother of Edith, is about 70 years old but dresses as if 27, with a false complexion and a faded manner; she is moved in a wheeled chair by her page. She is in reduced circumstances but makes much of being related to a lord. She is ambitious: years ago she pushed her daughter into marriage with a much older army officer when she was only a teenager because the man was a colonel (Edith's husband and a child of the marriage died not long after).

In Leamington she meets Major Bagstock, who introduces her to Mr Dombey; she flirts with the major as a "false creature" and a "perfidious goblin" but is quick to invite the two men to visit her.

Bagstock praises Edith's beauty to Dombey and Dombey's wealth to the women; Mrs Skewton starts scheming. When the engagement is made, Edith reproaches her mother for having always urged material motives and forced her to abandon natural feelings. The mother never notices Edith's distaste for the entire venture and rejoices in the union.

She remains ecstatic when the Dombeys are back from honeymoon and sees nothing but what she wants to see. She has a stroke but continues to dress in extravagantly youthful clothes. A second stroke, and she dies soon afterwards: Dombey sees to a Brighton funeral, attended by the deceased's distinguished relative, Lord Feenix.

TOODLE, ROBIN (II), eldest son of the numerous Toodle family: the father is a stoker on the new railways, the mother Polly is appointed nurse to little Paul Dombey. As a gesture to the family, Mr Dombey pays for the eldest boy to be educated at a school called the Charitable Grinders, but he is bullied and, unhappy, runs away, becoming a drifter known as Rob the Grinder, much given to self-pity.

He gets into bad company, and Carker the Manager employs him as a spy on the Dombey family's movements. In the end Rob reforms, is once again called Robin and becomes Miss Tox's manservant.

TOOTS, Mr P. (XI), head boy at Blimber's boarding school in Brighton. A tall teenager, mentally backward but endlessly patient and kind-hearted; by staff and pupils he is generally regarded as Paul's "protector and guardian". He leaves Blimber's as he has inherited wealth.

A week after Paul's funeral Toots, who has taken the trouble to wear deep mourning, visits Florence and makes her a present of the Blimber dog Diogenes.

He develops a habit of seeking contact with Florence; when told she is not available for whatever reason his standard diffident response is: "It's of no consequence".

On the day of the Dombey wedding he dresses as smartly as if he were a bridegroom himself to slip into a gallery of the church and watch the ceremony, and tells his friend, "Miss Dombey is the object of my passion".

Permanently in "a state of adoration" he seeks friendship with Captain Cuttle as a way to keep Florence fresh in his memory. When she goes to Brighton he plucks up courage to meet her and is about to make a declaration when she, knowing what is coming, gently dissuades him. He quickly replies: "It's of no consequence".

When Susan Nipper is dismissed for pleading Florence's cause with Mr Dombey, Florence asks Toots to take Susan to the night-coach. As she leaves he asks Susan if he thinks that Florence "could be brought to love me". Susan tells him never and he replies: "It's of no consequence".

Time goes by and he marries Susan, who slips back into her old job as Florence's maid.

TOX, LUCRETIA (I), spinster in reduced circumstances, friend of Mrs Chick, practised at being obsequious and flattering to everyone who she feels might be of use, harbouring thoughts about Mr Dombey after he has lost his wife.

To please Dombey, she eagerly does research on where to find a suitable nurse for the new Dombey baby and proudly produces the woman who gets the job, Polly Toodle.

When Mrs Chick tells her that Dombey is to remarry, Miss Tox faints and is denounced by Mrs Chick for harbouring the very ambitions which Mrs Chick had encouraged.

As the years go by, Miss Tox stays in contact with the Dombey domestic staff to hear how the family is faring. And after the fall of the House of Dombey she takes in one of the casualties, the youth Robin Toodle, reformed now after going wrong in the past and acting as a spy for James Carker; she makes him her attendant.

She goes to see the Gay family and Florence's father regularly; her feelings for the old man have become platonic.

GREAT EXPECTATIONS

DRUMMLE, BENTLEY (XXV), a rich and heavily built youth, a "contemptible, clumsy, sulky, booby", marries Estella. The marriage is unhappy; he is killed after mistreating a horse.

GARGERY, JOE (II), village blacksmith, a "mild, sweet-tempered …foolish dear fellow with curls of flaxen hair", strong in body but not in mind, much put upon by his wife as the household has its "squally times". Miss Havisham pays for Pip to be his apprentice; the indentures are cancelled when Pip gets his "Great Expectations". His resolution to keep loyally in touch with Joe is never carried out.

When Magwitch dies and Pip's Great Expectations have come to naught, Joe comes in to pay his outstanding debts and Pip tells him how ungrateful and disloyal he has been. At last he accords Joe the love and affection that is his due.

When Pip comes back after 11 years in the East he finds Joe happily married to his old friend Biddy; in the corner of the living room sits another little boy who looks just like Pip looked years ago: it is their son, also called Pip.

GARGERY, MRS JOE (II), Pip's married sister, more than 20 years older, is tall, bony with black hair, black eyes and a red face, dominating her husband and her timid little brother with her fierce temper. She regards herself "as a slave with her apron never off" and physically bullies them both. She is left brain-damaged from an attack by Joe's resentful journeyman Orlick and requires constant attention until she dies a few years later.

***HAVISHAM, ESTELLA (VIII)**, Miss Havisham's adopted daughter, "proud and self-possesed"; a teenager who acts as if she is 21 and when told by Miss Havisham to play cards with Pip is patronising and scornful of his clothes and his manner. She makes a habit of calling him "boy".

At the end of the game Estella serves him with bread and beer in such a humiliating way that tears come into his eyes; "she looked at me with a quick delight in having been the cause of them". From then he tries to hide his feelings out of pride but as he leaves the house she tells him that she knows he has "been crying until you are half blind" and laughs contemptuously.

They play cards when Pip visits Miss Havisham again. Miss Havisham watches Estella's changes of mood and tells her "break their hearts, my pride and hope, break their hearts and have no mercy". (Miss Havisham was abandoned by her groom on their wedding day.)

When Pip has moved to London to be educated for his new life, he goes back to his old haunts to visit Miss Havisham and finds Estella now a fine woman, "proud and wilful as of old", qualities "brought into subjection to her beauty". She tells Pip: "You must know that I have no hear t… sympathy – sentiment – nonsense."

When she goes to stay in Richmond, Pip visits her and finds her as capricious and dismissive as ever; she reaffirms that she does as she was taught by Miss Havisham. She admits to Pip that she is intends "to deceive and entrap" Drummle, and later tells him she will marry him.

Pip goes to dine with Mr Jaggers and notices a curious resemblance between his maidservant and Estella. Her history comes out: having had a daughter, Estella's mother was had up for murder and Jaggers as her defence solicitor got her off; she has been in service in his household ever since. Her child went to Miss Havisham and was adopted.

After his return from the East he meets Estella again, no longer the young beauty but with "indescribable majesty … and charm".

They talk and Pip ends his story: "I saw no shadow of another parting from her."

***HAVISHAM, MISS (VIII)**, elderly woman deserted by a fortune-hunter on her wedding day many years before and has never left the rooms in which the wedding was to have been celebrated. She lives in her gloomy mansion, Satis House, with a young companion, Estella.

In her cobwebbed quarters she wears a faded bridal gown in which her figure has become emaciated; the finery and wedding accoutrements have all turned yellow with "this standing still of all the pale decayed objects"; the clocks have all stopped at 20 minutes to nine, the time at which she got the letter in which her lover dismissed her. The man was in apparent collusion with her half-brother, likewise one of dissolute habits. Both men have vanished.

Confined to a room she never leaves, she has asked her tenant Pumblechook to bring her "a boy to play with". Pip arrives and he is told about her broken heart and commanded to play cards with Estella, the girl adopted by Miss Havisham.

The second time he visits her she takes him to the adjoining bridal party chamber where he sees the musty bride-cake. She watches Estella and Pip play cards and tells Estella to "break their hearts and have no mercy".

She pays a premium to Joe Gargery to take Pip on as an apprentice at his forge. In gratitude Pip visits her on his birthday each year.

Pip visits her when he goes to London and when he has settled down in Hammersmith. She rejoices in seeing him with the now-adult Estella and urges him to love her.

When he discovers that his real benefactor is Magwitch, not Miss Havisham, he goes to see her for the last time and she admits she misled him in thinking it was her doing. He leaves but turns back and finds she has set herself on fire by sitting too close to a fireplace; he smothers the flames with a greatcoat, saving her, but she dies later.

JAGGERS, MR (XVI), London solicitor with dark complexion, deep-set eyes and bushy black eyebrows, comes to the Gargerys' village and tells Joe and Pip that an unknown person has decided to endow Pip with Great Expectations; education, an ample income and a large estate on condition he never seeks to know who his benefactor is. Mr Jaggers, who as Miss Havisham's solicitor manages her affairs, will become Pip's official guardian.

Pip travels to the solicitor's office in Smithfield to begin his new life and finds Jaggers to be a hard-driving and hard-drinking man (sherry) who overawes all who come into contact with him, but he is always sternly protective of his ward.

***MAGWITCH, ABEL (I), a young convict who escapes from a prison ship on the Kent marshes, is starving and wet through when he confronts young Pip and frightens him with dire threats to get him food and a file to cut loose "the great iron on his leg".

Pip brings him bread, brandy and a pork pie but says there is no more where that came from. The convict is upset when he hears that another prisoner has escaped and is at large on the marshes.

A military search party comes to the village to look for the refugees. Joe and Pip follow the chase. Both convicts are found; Pip meets the eye of the young man he helped: "I slightly moved my hands and shook my head"; the man understands Pip did not betray him.

Both men are returned to the prison hulk; the first is Magwitch, the other Compeyson, but their names and significance are not revealed until much later.

Years later, when Pip is 23 (Chapter XXXIX), Magwitch risks his life to come back from New South Wales to see his protégée Pip; he is a worn grey man looking 60 years old who tells Pip he has prospered and that he was the secret source of Pip's "Great Expectations"; he also reveals his name, Abel Magwitch.

Pip's whole world and the structure he had built up around Miss Havisham and Estella have been overturned. He is also frightened because if Magwitch were found he would be hanged – convicts transported for life were forbidden to return to England.

Magwitch tells Pip and Herbert his life story; the man with whom he was sentenced to transportation was a confidence trickster called Compeyson – the man who deserted Miss Havisham on her wedding day and who was also on the marshes that day.

Magwitch confides about his early life; it turns out he is Estella's father, but does not know.

Pip and Herbert try to get him out of the country to safety. Their little boat, in which they go down the river to Gravesend to link with a paddle-steamer that will take him to the Continent, is trailed by a skiff carrying Magwitch's old enemy, Compeyson, and draws alongside; Magwitch and Compeyson grapple and wrestle in the water. Magwitch is hauled out badly injured and promptly manacled; Compeyson is later found drowned.

Magwitch is taken to court and despite defence pleas by Jaggers is sentenced to death. He is gravely ill and kept in the prison infirmary. He weakens; Pip tells him that he has a daughter who is a lady and very beautiful and (Pip adds) "I love her". Magwitch takes Pip's hand, kisses it and dies.

★★★**PIP (PHILIP PIRRIP) (I)**, the hero: his long-dead parents had seven children, two of whom survived: a daughter who grew up to marry the blacksmith Gargery and is always known as Mrs Joe, and one little son, Pip, 20 years her junior. Pip lives with his sister and her husband.

On a winter day, Pip goes out wandering near his home in a Kent village "in marsh country, down by the river … twenty miles off the sea", is surprised by "a fearful man all in coarse grey with a great iron on his leg" and wet through.

He "limped and shivered with his teeth chattering", treats Pip roughly and demands he produces food and a file because if he does not he will tear the little boy's heart and liver out. Terrified, Pip runs home. His sister is shrewish and he and his brother-in-law "share a freemasonry as fellow-sufferers". He is even more terrified now he has to secrete from the parsimonious household the food he has promised.

A gun is heard to go off; Mrs Joe tells him that it comes from a prison-hulk, where people are put "because they murder and rob and forge and do all things bad"; the gun is a sign a prisoner has escaped.

Pip brings the convict his file and "wittles" but with the risks he has taken tells him he cannot do it again. When the convict is taken they meet eyes and the convict realises that Pip has not betrayed him.

Joe's uncle, Pumblechook, takes Pip to Miss Havisham, who has asked him to bring a boy to play in her house. After he has played cards with Estella, the girl who lives there, he confesses to Miss Havisham that the girl is very pretty but insulting and that he would like to go home. Estella brings him food and beer in such a way that he cries and she makes no secret of her pleasure. Without self-pity Pip reflects that he is surrounded by unkindness and injustice.

He visits Miss Havisham again. She takes him into an adjoining room, where he sees a dusty festive table and a bride-cake covered with cobwebs. She tells him this is her birthday and that she will be laid out on this table when she is dead.

When he leaves her and finds himself in another part of the building, he is challenged to a fight by "a pale young gentleman with light hair", apparently his own age but taller.

The youth slaps him to give him reason for fighting and when they do Pip gives him a black eye and bloody nose. The youth acknowledges defeat.

Pip says goodbye to Estella, who capriciously says that he may kiss her – he does so realising there is no warmth.

He visits again. And plays cards again. Miss Havisham watches them play and follows Estella's changes of mood, to "embrace her with lavish fondness" and whisper to her "break their hearts, my pride and hope, break their hearts and have no mercy".

Pip grows up. Miss Havisham speaks of him entering into an apprenticeship and Joe is summoned to visit her. She gives him 25 guineas as a premium and tells Pip he need not come any more.

Pip starts working for Joe, unhappy with the coaldust and the "curtain dropped so heavy and blank" when he thought of his past experiences. There is only one relief: he is constantly touched by the influence of the "amiable, honest-hearted duty-doing" Joe, who is always kind to him. Even so, he cannot get away from the lasting impressions made on him by Miss Havisham and the moody, beautiful Estella.

He regularly visits Miss Havisham on his birthday and always receives a guinea from her. He is told that Estella is abroad to widen her education. Miss Havisham asks: "Do you feel that you have lost her?" and he notes in her voice the "malignant enjoyment".

With Mrs Joe handicapped by her assailant, a kindly girl from the village called Biddy who gave Pip his first lessons moves into the forge household to help run matters.

Pip and Biddy become friendly: he confesses to her that he does not like his trade and wants to become a gentleman. He speaks of Estella and says: "I admire her dreadfully and want to be a gentleman on her account." He also feels this desire is "very mad and misplaced" and admits that Biddy is a more worthy friend.

In the fourth year of his apprenticeship he is visited by Jaggers, a solicitor who draws Pip and Joe aside and tells them privately that he is empowered to say that Pip has "Great Expectations", that he will come into handsome property and should be removed "from his present sphere of life ... and be brought up as a gentleman – in a word, as a young fellow of great expectations".

Pip tells himself immediately: "My dream was out; my wild

fancy was surpassed by sober reality; Miss Havisham was going to make my fortune on a grand scale."

He is told of some conditions: he must always refer to himself as Pip and never seek to know the identity of his benefactor; Jaggers will be his guardian from now on; he will be placed with a tutor, one Matthew Pocket, a name which Pip has heard of previously as a relative of Miss Havisham's.

Pip travels to London and is escorted by Mr Jaggers's clerk Wemmick to the dingy Barnard's Inn rooms of Matthew Pocket's son Herbert, who turns out to be friendly – and is the "pale young gentleman" whom Pip thrashed in a flight at Miss Havisham's years ago.

Pip goes to live with Herbert's father, Matthew, a cousin of Miss Havisham's, who will be his tutor. Matthew and his disorganised noisy family live in Hammersmith; there are two other lodgers, Drummle and Startop.

Pip's years in the smithy have made him a strong young man: he knocked down Herbert Pocket years ago and in his Hammersmith stay becomes a forceful enough oarsman on the tidal Thames to be a match for Startop and leave the other boarder Drummle well behind.

Pip visits Miss Havisham and meets Estella, back from France. He reflects: "I loved Estella with the love of a man … against hope against happiness, against all discouragement that could be." He is struck by her beauty and hauteur.

On returning to London he confides in Herbert how he loves Estella and Herbert gently – and ineffectually – suggests it may be wise to look elsewhere for love.

When Joe's wife dies and Pip goes to the funeral he resolves to visit Joe regularly and comfort him – again knowing that he will not get round to doing so.

On the day that Pip becomes 21, Jaggers gives him a bank-note for £500 as a present and tells him that from now on he will have an allowance of £500 a year, payable in quarterly instalments from the clerk Wemmick.

Without Herbert's knowledge he arranges through Wemmick to give his young friend an opening with a shipping-broker in the City; privately he sheds tears that at last he can do some good with his money.

When Pip is 23 he is visited in his new quarters in the Temple by a grey-haired weather-beaten man who expresses delight at meeting him.

It is the convict Magwitch, who has prospered in New South Wales, has devoted his business success to giving Pip his "Great Expectations" and has risked his life to come and see Pip: "I'm your second father".

Pip is appalled and frightened. His dreams about the supposed generosity of Miss Havisham and the prospect of winning Estella's love have been overturned; also, the visitor hiding in his quarters would be hanged if he were found: convicts were forbidden from returning from Australia.

Magwitch tells Pip and Herbert his life story: how he started badly in life and fell in with even worse company, including a man called Arthur who was the lost half-brother of Miss Havisham. Arthur's companion in crime was a confidence trickster called Compeyson – the gentlemanly crook who deserted Miss Havisham on her wedding day. Magwitch and Compeyson were both sentenced to transportation for passing stolen bank-notes.

Pip goes to see Miss Havisham, who admits she allowed him to think she was his benefactress; he confesses his life-long love to Estella, who says she warned him off long ago: anyway, she is to marry Drummle. Pip protests in vain against her giving herself to "a mean brute, such a stupid brute". She dismisses Pip as "you visionary boy".

At the end of another visit he says his goodbyes, but turns back and finds Miss Havisham, having sat too near a fire, enveloped in flames. He saves her by wrapping her emaciated body in a greatcoat; he himself has severe arm burns and is lovingly tended by Herbert.

Pip, no longer using Magwitch's money, persuades Miss Havisham to pay £900 to further Herbert's business career, help he himself would have given. The money goes to Herbert's firm, Clarriker's, which decides to send the young man to their business in the East, much to his delight. Pip himself is happy, too – "the only good thing I had done, and the only completed thing I had done".

Pip and Herbert try to get Magwitch to safety on a boat making for the Continent but they are caught by the authorities who have Compeyson with them. Magwitch, gravely injured in grappling with Compeyson, is brought ashore and sentenced to death, and taken to the prison infirmary. Pip realises at last that he loves his benefactor.

With Magwitch weak and failing, Pip tells him that he has a daughter who is very beautiful "and I love her". Magwitch kisses Pip's hand and dies. With Magwitch's assets reverting to the Crown, Pip has no resources. Joe Gargery steps in to pay his outstanding debts and tends to him as he lies ill with fever. Here, too, Pip gives Joe at last his due in love and affection.

Pip goes to join his friend Herbert in a new career in the East, and comes back after 11 years, having prospered modestly. He finds Joe happily married to Biddy; they have a son they have called Pip.

In the gardens where Miss Havisham's house once stood, later that day he meets Estella, now a widow, the freshness of her beauty gone but the "indescribable majesty … and charm remained". He tells her: "You have always held a place in my heart." She replies: "Be as considerate and good to me as you were, and tell me we are friends". He takes her hand and "I saw no shadow of another parting from her".

★★★POCKET, HERBERT (XXII), is the young man who Pip visits as his new London life begins. Herbert lives in dismal quarters in Barnard's Inn, a young man without much drive, but he is friendly and outgoing; it turns out he was the young man whom Pip beat in a fight at Miss Havisham's years ago. The young men know that Pip is never to inquire who his benefactor is but as Herbert's father is Miss Havisham's cousin they presume it is all Miss Havisham's doing.

Through the agency of Wemmick, Pip arranges that Herbert is given a job with a shipping broker in the City called Clarriker, which excites him as giving him at last "his opening in life", but he does not know that Pip and Wemmick engineered this.

On his last visit to Miss Havisham, Pip pleads that (having returned his own fortune) she pay £900 towards further development of his friend Herbert's career. She agrees. With it his firm Clarriker's will send him to the East; Herbert is very happy and still does not know that Pip was responsible. It is on Herbert's initiative that Pip begins a new business career in the East.

POCKET, MATTHEW (XXIII), father of Herbert, is appointed Pip's tutor with whom Pip is to live. He is the head of a chaotic family with a house in Hammersmith. He is Miss Havisham's cousin, who at the end of the story is left £4,000 in her will.

Pip and two other lodgers with Pocket senior, Drummle and Startop, all have a boat on the river: Pip goes half-share with his new friend Herbert Pocket, with whom he regularly goes to stay. Thanks to his work in the smithy Pip has strong arms and turns out to be a successful oarsman.

PUMBLECHOOK, MR (IV), Joe's uncle and a well-to-do corn chandler, a "large hard-breathing middle-aged slow man with a mouth like a fish and dull staring eyes". A pompous overbearing man, he rents property from a Miss Havisham, "an immensely rich and grim lady" who lives a life of seclusion. She has asked her tenant to bring her a boy to play with; Pumblechook sends Pip.

At the end of the story Pumblechook's home is well and truly stripped by the onetime Gargery journeyman-turned-burglar Orlick, who ends his career in jail.

WEMMICK, JOHN (XXI), clerk in Jaggers's chambers in his forties, a dry rather short man with "a square wooden face" and "glittering eyes, small, keen and black". His manner is reserved but when he invites Pip to his home in the suburb of Walworth he turns into a warm and kindly host devoted to his deaf father, the Aged Parent. It is a pleasant home; when they return to town Wemmick shuts up his personality again, explaining: "The Aged is one person and Mr Jaggers is another. They must not be confounded together."

Pip is best man when Wemmick marries his long-standing love Miss Skiffins.

HARD TIMES

***BLACKPOOL, STEPHEN (First Book, X)**, aged 40, power loom weaver in the tycoon Bounderby's mill in Coketown, has a stoop and iron-grey hair. Married to an alcoholic who periodically sells off his belongings for drink. He has a friend, mill worker Rachael, 35, who is kind and understanding.

Blackpool goes to his employer's home in a hopeless bid to see if he can get a divorce and marry Rachael.

A trade union organiser comes to Coketown and fires up the workers, except for Stephen, who warns against such a confrontational manner towards employers: as a result his colleagues send Stephen to Coventry – and when he tries gently to explain to Bounderby, too, that a confrontational approach between employers and employees is inadvisable, Bounderby sacks him. He packs a small bundle of belongings and leaves Coketown.

After the bank robbery Bounderby puts up posters offering a reward of £20 for finding him as a possible suspect. On his way back to Coketown to put matters straight, Stephen falls down a disused mine shaft (Old Hell Shaft) and is discovered by Sissy and Rachael. He is pulled clear; Gradgrind is among the people called to the scene and he pleads with the MP: "Yo will clear me an' mak my name good wi' all men… yor son will tell yo how. Ask him, I mak no charges." He asks Rachael to hold his hand and he dies. Gradgind provides a decent tombstone for him.

***BOUNDERBY, JOSIAH (First Book, V)**, aged 47 or 48, self-made merchant and manufacturer, "a man made of coarse material" "with a stare and a metallic laugh", proclaims he was born in a ditch "ragged and dirty" and learned to read from shop signs, "pulled himself up from vagabond to becoming Bounderby of Coketown", also in his manner proclaims "his ignorance and his poverty, a Bully of humanity".

He marries Lousia Gradgrind, who is 30 years his junior. The marriage is a loveless arrangement and she is emotionally starved. When James Harthouse with his smooth manners comes to stay as a house guest and exploits her isolated situation she falls for him and he urges elopement: on the evening of flight Louisa pulls back and returns to her father's house, where Bounderby comes to expostulate.

Gradgrind suggests a period of calm reassessment while Louisa stays with him for a while (he is now a widower). Bounderby blusteringly refuses, gives Louisa a deadline for her prompt return and when it expires the next day sends her belongings back, advertises "his country retreat for sale by private contract and resumed a bachelor life".

An elderly woman brought to Bounderby's house is revealed to be his mother: so far from his having the rough background he always spoke of, the family was respectable and loving in an orderly household; his mother was proud of his progress and grateful for the secret allowance he made her of £30 a year – provided she stayed away from him. Bounderby is reduced to "blustering sheepishness"; he is "crestfallen and superlatively absurd". He dies of a fit in a Coketown street five years later.

GRADGRIND, LOUISA (First Book, III), oldest child of Thomas Gradgrind, is upbraided by her father at the start of the story for looking at a circus and not concentrating on facts. As she grows up she is so well schooled that she learns well to mask gentler feelings.

When she is 20 a loveless marriage is arranged between her and her father's friend Bounderby, a businessman now aged 50; she makes herself "impassive proud and cold, holding (even her friend) Sissy at a distance".

After a year of marriage she is "small and slight but very graceful", warm only to her brother, who has become a wastrel.

She sees Blackpool curtly dismissed by her husband and comes after him and lends him money to help him along.

James Harthouse comes from London at her father's instigation to stay with the Bounderbys; he quickly senses Louisa's emotional isolation and ingratiates himself with her by pretending to be solicitous about her brother.

She gradually responds but when he urges her to come away she flees to her father's house and tells him how she has been emotionally crippled by her upbringing: "… you have doomed me … to the frost and blight that have hardened and spoiled me". He responds gently; she is comforted by her sister Jane and the long-faithful Sissy.

After Blackpool dies and Tom is helped to escape abroad she does not remarry but becomes much loved by Sissy's numerous family.

***GRADGRIND, THOMAS (First Book, I)**, aged about 50, headmaster and teacher, squarely built, with a "mouth that is wide, thin and hard set", bristly hair, tells his pupils that all they have to learn is fact, not fancy.

He is a former hardware wholesaler, now a teacher, and has his sights on going into Parliament. He has built his home Stone Lodge on a moor a mile or two from Coketown, a redbrick industrial city. His five children are Louisa, Thomas, Jane, Adam Smith and Malthus, "all lectured at from their tenderest years". Bounderby is his closest friend.

He upbraids one of his pupils, Sissy Jupe, for suggesting in class that she might furnish a room with a carpet representing flowers and goes to the local circus, to which she apparently belongs, to tell the circus master she is not suitable to be a pupil. It turns out that Sissy's father has just run away; it is agreed that she will go and live with the Gradgrind household and she takes a tearful farewell of the friendly circus folk.

Gradgrind's children grow up, his wife remains sickly and browbeaten, and he becomes an MP.

Time passes. When he comes back from the Commons to Coketown his daughter comes home a few hours later and tells him that she has fled from elopement with Harthouse, a man she fell for because he had shown her kindness which her father – and husband – never had. Gradgrind hears her reproaches and is repentant and understanding.

After Blackpool's death his son confesses to him that he stole the money and he helps Tom to flee abroad. Louisa living with him, he is now "a white-haired decrepit man … making his facts and figures subservient to Faith, Hope and Charity".

GRADGRIND, THOMAS (First Book, III), son of Thomas Gradgrind, is sternly schooled by his father and takes naturally to becoming self-centred and self-seeking. When he leaves school he is given a job in Bounderby's Bank, becomes a "dissolute" and a "hyprocrite", is ungracious even to his sister but borrows heavily from her to go gambling and tells his new friend Harthouse that he is in financial trouble and blames his sister for not helping.

The bank is robbed; £150 is missing. Tom lets suspicion fall on the now-jobless Blackpool and the outraged Bounderby takes this up. Louisa goes to her brother and asks him if there is anything he could tell her but he stays silent, but in the coming weeks stays quietly by Bounderby's side.

Sissy hears what Blackpool says to Gradgrind before he dies about his son, and urges Tom to flee. Sissy and Louisa find him in Sleary's circus where Sissy lived in earlier times; Tom confesses to his father that he forced the safe to steal the money; he is helped to go abroad where he eventually writes to his sister and wishes he could see her again. On his way back to England he catches a fever and "dies in penitence and love of you".

HARTHOUSE, JAMES (Second Book, II), smooth-mannered upper-class drifter who wants to join the political world, is sent by Gradgrind MP to stay with the Bounderbys. He quickly notes their domestic situation and plays on the feelings of the emotion-starved Louisa.

The relationship develops; he wants to take her away. Instead, she goes to her father and Sissy Jupe comes to tell him that he will not meet Louisa again. He leaves the Bounderby house feeling ridiculous.

JUPE, SISSY (CECILIA) (First Book, II), a pupil at Mr Gradgrind's school, is taken in by the Gradgrind household as a kind of domestic after her father, a circus clown in Sleary's Circus, apparently abandons her. The change of scene, with a stern regimen and total loss of the affection with which she used to be surrounded, makes her deeply unhappy; she forms a kind of friendship with Gradgrind's eldest daughter, Louisa, who also has tender feelings but is better adapted to her loveless surroundings.

When Louisa comes home to her father, pulling back from elopement with Harthouse, she comforts her old friend and goes to tell the lover she has withdrawn.

The dying Blackpool urges Gradgrind to ask his son about the robbery. Sissy warns Tom to flee.

She marries and has children who become very fond of Louisa, who never remarries.

SPARSIT, MRS (First book, vii), impoverished gentlewoman employed as part of Mr Bounderby's household at £100 a year. She is highly connected to the aristocratic Lady Scadgers.

It is Bounderby's pleasure ceaselessly to contrast this "woman of good family" with his own background. To his face she is servile and sycophantic ("trouble in your service, sir, is to me a pleasure"); behind his back she makes waspish reference to "this Noddle". She gleefully spies on the growing intimacy between Louisa and

Harthouse and rushes to London to report to her employer but gets no thanks for her pains.

She finds Mrs Pegler, Bounderby's mother, thinking she is doing him a favour, but when Mrs Pegler's revelations show his deprived childhood was a myth he angrily dismisses Mrs Sparsit – who returns to live with Lady Scadgers.

LITTLE DORRIT

CASBY, CHRISTOPHER (XIII), former town agent to Lord Decimus Tite Barnacle and "by common report to be rich in house property", with his blue eyes, smooth face, silken locks and meek manner is said to be just like an old-fashioned patriarch; in fact he is a rent racketeer who lets his clerk Pancks do his collecting for him and upbraids him when he does not squeeze enough money from poor tenants in slum properties such as Bleeding Heart Yard. He has a daughter called Flora, once courted by Arthur Clennam before he went to China.

Arthur, grateful that Casby has called Little Dorrit in to do needlework for Flora, goes to see how his former love is – with disappointing results.

Pancks is angered when Casby tells him once too often that he should squeeze the tenants harder. He denounces his boss, takes shears and trims his hat as well the distinguished patriarchal locks; Casby is left "a blundering old booby".

CAVALETTO, JOHN BAPTIST (I), held in a Marseilles prison cell on a smuggling charge, a "quick lithe little man with earrings and white teeth", has earrings and a red cap. He is good-natured and his manner reveals "easy contentment with hardship". He finds the criminal Rigaud, with whom he is sharing his cell, frightening.

On his release he makes his way to London and is taken under the wing of Arthur Clennam, who supports him financially. Cavaletto is found a room in Bleeding Heart Yard and has a new career carving flowers and as caretaker of the Doyce and Clennam premises.

CHIVERY, JOHN (XVIII), teenage son of a Marshalsea turnkey, is a small man with "weak light hair". He has for years been in love with Little Dorrit, who is of his own age, and has known her all his life. When he plucks up courage to make a declaration to her she is troubled and does not allow him to speak.

When William Dorrit returns to London in his rich days, John diffidently come to visit him to give him cheap cigars as a kindly reminder of the old days. William is at first outraged at this reminder of his past, but mellows and gives John a cheque for £100 for the inmates of the Marshalsea.

After Arthur Clennam has been taken to the Marshalsea for debt, John visits him out of kindness and reveals that Little Dorrit, who he (Clennam) has always regarded as a special charge but no more, has secretly loved him for years.

★★★CLENNAM, ARTHUR (II), is returning home from 20 years of running a business in China. He and his father were sent abroad by his overbearing materialist mother and now that his father is dead he is 40 years old, is unattached and wants to start a new life back home. He has suffered disappointments in life but has a kind and helpful nature and remains a dreamer and idealist.

When the story opens, he is caught up in the quarantine imposed by the Marseilles authorities and makes friends with the Meagles family.

On his arrival at his mother's home in London dockland he is given a cool welcome and she heatedly denies his question whether the firm – from which he now wishes to withdraw – ever did anything to harm others as he sensed from his late father.

He sees Amy working unobtrusively in a corner in his mother's room. When asked who she is, the mother says: "That's just LITTLE DORRIT, a seamstress".

Amy's conduct attracts his attention and sympathy: he asks himself whether his firm had a role in the fall of the Dorrits, and is there a reason why his mother should uncharacteristically be more gentle in her attitude to Amy? In the course of the story it turns out that his suspicion is justified.

Little Dorrit confides in Arthur that her father's affairs are complex; the only place where the truth might be found would be in the Circumlocution Office in Grosvenor Square.

This is the "most important department under government", with fingers in every pie and which has a message for all departments when it comes to taking action: "how not to do it". It is run by two noble families who are big names in the land: the Tite Barnacles and the Stiltstalkings.

Arthur goes to the C.O. to find out about a Dorrit inheritance and is sent from pillar to post by various Tite Barnacles, who act as a brake on the functioning of the country.

Frustrated, he leaves the building and comes across his friend Mr Meagles, who is also irate because he is with yet another person who has just seen the non-workings of the C.O.; experienced engineer Daniel Doyce has been given the brush-off about his useful invention.

Arthur goes to see Mr Casby to thank him for giving Little Dorrit the chance to do needlework for his daughter Flora, so bolstering her small income, and stays on to see Casby's daughter Flora, to whom he was once engaged.

He meets her. Though he has remained an idealist, "his eyes no sooner fell upon the subject of his old passion, than it shivered and broke to pieces". She has grown to be very broad, and in her speech and manner is not just spoilt but "diffuse and silly".

He comes across a young man injured in a street accident and goes to help. It is the Italian Cavaletto; Clennam takes pity on him, finds him accommodation and agrees to support him.

Through Meagles, he and Doyce set up a partnership called Doyce and Clennam in which Doyce will handle the technical side and Clennam starts a new career looking after the business.

Pancks tells Arthur that he has discovered that the Dorrits are "heir-at-law to a great fortune". Arthur thinks Amy should be the first to know and finds her at Flora's. He tells her – Amy promptly faints.

When the family leave the Marshalsea in a fleet of fine carriages the cry goes up: where is Little Dorrit?

She has been forgotten by her closest relatives: the faithful Arthur goes back into the prison and finds her overwhelmed and insensible. He takes her in his arms and carries her out.

The Dorrits collect their money and leave for the Continent. Arthur misses the neglected younger daughter: he has always looked on her as "his innocent friend, his delicate child". He reads avidly her letters from Italy signed "Little Dorrit".

When on a visit to his mother he sees Rigaud there as well, he protests and she asks her son to leave. Later that night Rigaud is seen leaving Mrs Clennam's warehouse but then vanishes; this worries Arthur.

Because he had earlier seen Rigaud with Miss Wade and Tattycoram, he traces the two women to a cheap lodging in Calais and asks what they might know about him. Miss Wade coldly says she used Rigaud simply to fetch her money from Casby's office; she knows nothing more about him.

Arthur learns from his little Italian friend Cavaletto that this sinister man they both know was in a Marseilles prison on a murder charge. Arthur goes to his mother to warn her – she says it has nothing to do with her.

Merdle's suicide and the collapse of the Merdle empire lands Arthur in crisis: he invested all Doyce's money in Merdle and with that now lost he has transferred to Doyce what little he has himself. Thus he is now penniless and taken to the Marshalsea for debt.

Another shock: the turnkey son John Chivery reveals that Little Dorrit, whom Arthur has always regarded as a special charge, has secretly loved him for years.

Arthur lingers on in the Marshalsea, gravely ill because of his confinement and his feeling of guilt at having let Doyce down; he is constantly visited by Little Dorrit.

Doyce comes back having prospered abroad, waves away the misjudgement whereby Arthur lost all his money and says he again needs a partner anyway.

The firm of Doyce and Clennam is resuscitated and this gives Arthur the status and freedom to leave the Marshalsea. Doyce is best man when Arthur marries Amy Dorrit; the couple go on to lead "a modest life of usefulness and happiness".

★★★**CLENNAM, MRS (I)**, mother of Arthur Clennam, humourless dominatrix, lives in a gloomy warehouse by the Thames that has for years been both her business headquarters and her home. She has long been confined to her wheelchair; she is joylessly pious, with "cold grey eyes and cold grey hair". She is dependent on two live-in retainers, Jeremiah Flintwinch (a "little keen-eyed crab-like old man") and his wife, Affery.

Arthur arrives after 20 years of separation: she gives him a chilly welcome and reads from her Bible. He tells her that the business has been running down for years; another firm has taken over what is left and with his father's death it now has so little to do that he wants to pull out altogether.

He reminds her that his father went to China because she told him to, and that her child followed him there when he was 20. He adds, "In grasping at money and driving hard bargains, some may have been grievously deceived, injured, ruined." He asks her if this is true because he suspected as much in his father's manner.

She rages at him and calls Flintwinch in to deny that any such thing happened. She immediately appoints Flintwinch as her business partner to replace her son.

The adventurer Rigaud, also known as Blandois, twice visits Mrs Clennam and says he has business to propose.

On the second occasion Arthur is present and pleads with his mother that this man is not suitable company and she asks her son to leave.

Rigaud vanishes in curious circumstances and Arthur, apart

from seeking him himself, commissions Cavaletto to help seek find him. By the time he is found Arthur is in the Marshalsea and Rigaud visits him there. Arthur explains angrily: "How dare you direct a suspicion of murder against my mother's house?" Rigaud said he was after a business project with the House of Clennam; he writes from Arthur's cell giving Mrs Clennam another week to do a deal.

Rigaud arrives at the agreed time and demands £2,000 for a family secret and the background to the Clennams comes out:

An elderly uncle, Gilbert Clennam, had a weak nephew, Arthur's father, intended for a strong-minded woman who would make something of him – the woman who became Mrs Clennam. Earlier on, Arthur's father had had an affair with a singer in Frederick Dorrit's café and had a son by her. He then married as planned, foisting on his strong-minded wife his illegitimate son, Arthur.

Gilbert made a codicil to his will leaving a fortune to Little Dorrit as the niece of his friend Frederick Dorrit. This is the paper that Mrs Clennam held back from Arthur, whom she brought up as her own because she felt herself "an instrument of severity against sin".

Rigaud threatens that unless she pays up he will expose her. With a great effort Mrs Clennam – after having been chairbound for years, leaves her room and walks across London to reach Little Dorrit in the Marshalsea. She confesses what she has done, and begs for forgiveness.

She asks that Amy come back with her to tell Rigaud his threat is now meaningless. Amy readily agrees; the two women walk back to the Clennam warehouse and arrive there just in time to see the building blow up with Rigaud inside.

The shock gives Mrs Clennam a stroke. She is paralysed for the next three years and "lives and dies a statue".

***DORRIT, AMY (V)**, generally known as **LITTLE DORRIT**, makes her characteristically unobtrusive entrance to a story (where in fact she is the central figure) crouched in the corner of Mrs Clennam's room, where she is employed to do needlework.

Son Arthur, on his first visit to his mother, asks who the little figure he happened to see in the corner is and she replies: "That's LITTLE DORRIT." As the story develops, he gets to realise that she is "a tender child in body, a strong heroine in soul".

Born in the Marshalsea debtors' prison, where her father has been a inmate for 23 years, Amy is the youngest of his three children and was born in the prison.

She is a "diminutive figure with small features, a slight spare dress, so little and light, so noiseless and shy". Although already in her twenties, she has "all the manner and much of the appearance of a subdued child". The pale transparent face is "quick in expression, though not beautiful in feature, its soft hazel eyes excepted".

She is her father William's shield and protectress, particularly since her mother died some years before. She brings him his meals and sees to it that his room is always comfortable. He is vaguely thankful for her help.

Amy has a feckless brother Edward ("Tip"), whom she has tried to place in various jobs without success and a sister who through Amy's initiative is now a dancer in a small theatre. As for Amy herself, she won over a milliner to teach her to become "a cunning needlewoman" so she, too, can make a living.

The self-effacing Amy is in fact the mainstay of the family but gets no credit for it. This is Little Dorrit who, night after night, slips unobtrusively into the Marshalsea.

She also has a protégée: a slum girl called Maggy, who has a mental age of 10 and has attached herself to Amy, whom she calls "little mother".

Amy is working in Flora's room when Arthur comes to break the news that the family fortune has been recovered and that she will in future want for nothing; she faints.

And on the day of the family's departure from the Marshalsea she is forgotten by all the family – it is Arthur who goes back, finds her unconscious and carries her in his arms to the waiting carriage, still in her shabby dress.

She accompanies her family on the journey; "all she saw was new and wonderful, but it was not real". She is patronised, particularly by her sister, for her modesty and withdraws into herself: "she had no-one to think for, nothing to plan and contrive".

Unlike her father and siblings, who glory in their new wealth and flaunt it constantly, she remains self-effacing and quiet, for which she is rebuked by her sister and father; her uncle Frederick breaks out to protest that this is hard on her.

She returns from Italy and goes to see Arthur, imprisoned in the Marshalsea for debt. She sees that his health is failing; he sees that she looks more womanly "and the ripening touch of the Italian sun was visible upon her face" but otherwise she has "the same deep, timid earnestness". She wears her old prison dress and takes out her needlework case to make a curtain for the window of his cell.

Mrs Clennam, on the night Rigaud comes to threaten her with exposure, makes a great effort to reach Little Dorrit and forestall him by telling her about the codicil in the Clennam uncle's will which left her a fortune. Mrs Clennam confesses: "I will restore to you what I have withheld from you. Forgive me!"

She confesses more: she gave Amy work to do in her living room not out of compassion but to ease her conscience – she had been an "instrument of severity against sin".

She pleads with Amy to come back with her and tell her blackmailer that the secret is out anyway. Little Dorrit agrees; together they walk to the warehouse and arrive just in time to see it blow up.

With Arthur ill and in such a predicament, Amy offers to lend him her fortune to get him out. He refuses: "I am disgraced enough, my Little Dorrit." She leaves sending by young Chivery the message of her "undying love" for Arthur.

With the revival of the Doyce partnership and Arthur freed from the Marshalsea, Little Dorrit and Arthur Clennam are married and go on to live together a "modest life of usefulness and happiness".

DORRIT, FANNY (IX), Amy's elder sister, is a dancer in a cheap theatre. She is impetuous and superficial. Little Dorrit visits her and together the sisters go to an acquaintance of Fanny's, Mrs Merdle.

This haughty woman is a banker's wife burdened with a son, Edmund Sparkler, who has a weakness for proposing marriage to theatre girls. Mrs Merdle gives Fanny generous presents; Amy, shrewder than her sister, can tell this is a bribe to keep her out of the way but when she points this out she is abused for her pains.

Fanny takes to her new status and freedom in Italy with gusto and enourages once again the attentions of the weak-minded Sparkler, who, having been appointed to a post in the Circumlocution Office, marries her – and immediately she dominates him. In London as a married woman, Fanny glories in her new position.

She loses her money in the Merdle collapse but remains proud and "feeling deeply wronged".

DORRIT, FREDERICK (VIII), brother to Wiliam and uncle to Amy, is a professional clarinet player in the same small theatre where his other niece is a dancer. He has "a dim eye, palsied hand and … groping mind". He is always dirty and meanly dressed, humble and subdued, shuffles along carrying the limp case containing his instrument. He is patronised by William as if William has created his career rather than bringing ruin upon him.

Coming in to their newfound wealth, in Rome he breaks out of his customary reticence to protest vehemently to his brother when Wiliam and his elder daughter criticise Amy for refusing to change her modest ways.

When William dies Frederick is overcome with grief and dies kneeling by his brother's deathbed.

***DORRIT, WILLIAM (VI)**, father of Little Dorrit, was thrown into the Marshalsea for debt 23 years ago and now takes pride in being recognised by inmates and turnkeys as the longest resident, the Father of the Marshalsea. He is "amiable, well-looking but in an effeminate style".

Years ago he invested in a partnership and with no comprehension of business he still does not know what went wrong, but his incompetence brought ruin. Despite that, his manner is self-satisfied and imperturbably urbane.

On the day of their release from the Marshalsea, he leads the family procession hand in hand with Frederick. On the Italian journey his manner is grand and overbearing. He has hired as guide and chaperone a self-important widow, Mrs General, whose personality is "ample, rustling and gravely voluminous".

To the entire Dorrit party the accession of wealth and status has gone to their heads: the only exception is Little Dorrit herself, who remains modest and self-effacing, for which she is upbraided by her sister and father; Amy's uncle Frederick sees this and breaks out of his habitual silence to protest loudly at such treatment.

The adventurer Rigaud, now calling himself Blandois, attaches himself to the Dorrits and impresses them, but Amy and her new friend Pet Meagles (now Mrs Gowan) instinctively draw away.

William is portentously gratified by the marriage of Fanny to Sparkler; he turns to Little Dorrit and tells her now it is her turn. She tells him gently that there is no-one.

At a grand dinner he puzzles the rich and famous by going into raptures about his old life in the Marshalsea. A few days later he dies. The ever-loyal Frederick is overcome with grief and dies by his bedside. The brothers are buried together in Rome.

DOYCE, DANIEL (X), an engineer and inventor with experience in France, Germany and Russia, has come back to Britain with a useful invention for which he has been trying to attract government interest for 12 years. Instead, it has sent him from one department to another: now, with his visit to the Circumlocution Office, the quest has come to a frustrating end.

Doyce is a "timid gentle chap" who has become "older, sterner and poorer" through his experiences with officialdom though his technical skills are first-rate. The obfuscation in the C.O. annoys his friend Meagles, who wants to help press the matter further, as he explains to Arthur Clennam, who has also just come from the C.O. without success.

Meagles is instrumental in bringing the two men together to set up a business partnership, Doyce and Clennam, with offices in Bleeding Heart Yard. Partnership and friendship flourish.

Doyce goes abroad on business leaving Arthur in charge; they agree that Arthur should meanwhile continue the financial side of the business. While he is away Arthur invests all the firm's money in the Merdle enterprise just before the crash.

Doyce comes back to Britain having prospered. He is generous in forgiving Arthur for losing all his money but, having recovered his finances abroad, says he needs a partner again anyway, and Arthur is reinstated. The partnership flourishes, eventually taking in Pancks as well. Doyce is best man when Arthur marries Little Dorrit.

FINCHING, FLORA (XIII), courted in her youth by Arthur Clennam; the relationship was broken off when he went to China. She was married and widowed and now lives with her father, the racketeer Casby. Clennam visits her and is saddened to find that, although still good-natured and kind, she has become foolish and scatterbrained.

GOWAN, HENRY (XVII), a snob and would-be artist has been courting Pet Meagles, much to her parents' distress as they rightly feel he would make a poor husband.

On the wedding day, the greatest prize is that his cousin, Lord Decimus Tite Barnacle, "highest glory of the Barnacle family" and high in the Circumlocution Office, is there to propose the health of the bride and groom.

The Gowans happen to meet the Dorrits as they travel into Italy; the modest Amy befriends the modest Pet, while Henry Gowan and his new Dorrit friends relish their wealth and status.

The Gowans separate; he gets financial support from his father-in-law, she goes back to her parents with her son.

MEAGLES, MR (II), retired banker with "whimsical good humour", is held in quarantine with his family by the Marseilles authorities after visiting a plague territory.

He is travelling with his wife, "comely and healthy with a pleasant English face", their daughter Minnie ("Pet") and Pet's maid Tattycoram. They went abroad to get Pet away from a suitor her parents disapprove of, Gowan.

The Meagles are well-to-do, with a pleasant home on the banks of the Thames at Twickenham, to which they are returning from their travels. In Marseilles they make friends with Arthur Clennam and also meet another English traveller, Miss Wade.

When Mr Meagles visits Arthur, now a prisoner in the Marshalsea, he is suddenly confronted with Tattycoram, who has run away from Miss Wade, and begs for her old job back. As Pet Meagles has separated from Gowan and returned to her parents he is only too glad to welcome her.

Meagles has also found Doyce prospering in Arab countries and brought him back to Britain, leading to the firm of Doyce and Clennam being revived.

MEAGLES, MINNIE ("PET"), (II), "round and fresh and dimpled and spoilt", is the Meagles' only surviving child. About 20 with rich brown hair and an affectionate manner. Pet is in love with the pretentious artist Gowan and the foreign journey had the aim of getting him out of her mind.

She marries Gowan and on their European tour meets the Dorrit family. Henry Gowan remains offhand to her; she forms a friendship with Amy Dorrit – both of them modest and retiring people – and at Amy's request always calls her Little Dorrit. Pet has a son, the marriage breaks up and she returns to her parents.

★★★**MERDLE, MR (XXI)**, banker with a fine house in Harley Street, and held in society to wield enormous influence, gives a dinner attended by magnates directors, financiers and bishops and is flattered and fawned on by everyone. The word goes round to the public, even to the poor in Bleeding Heart Yard, that this Merdle investment opportunity is too good to miss. Rumours circulate that he has refused a baronetcy and will settle for nothing less than a peerage.

Of a summer evening Mr Merdle calls unexpectedly at the town house of his stepson Sparkle and asks to borrow a penknife. Next morning he is found in a blood-stained bath with a self-inflicted injury. His death ruins many.

MERDLE, MRS (XX), is a large woman "not young and fresh from Nature but from the hand of her maid". She has "large unfeeling handsome eyes and a broad unfeeling handsome bosom". She gives Fanny Dorrit presents to keep her away from her son.

When Fanny does become her daughter-in-law she and Fanny, both being snobs, skirt politely around the fact that Fanny is a onetime dancing girl.

After the collapse of the Merdle empire, the widow continues to shine in society by running down her husband in death as she did during his lifetime.

PANCKS (XIII), a dingy "quick and eager short dark man" with a manner like a little harbour tug; he has two sides to him; for his employer Casby he is a ruthless rent collector careless of the hardship he causes.

Privately, however, he happens to discover the hidden Dorrit inheritance which gets William freed from Marshalsea prison.

He is depressed by the loss of all his savings in the Merdle crash and when his employer Casby upbraids him again for not squeezing the poor tenants hard enough he turns and assaults his boss and walks out. He later becomes first a clerk and then a partner in the resuscitated firm of Doyce and Clennam.

RIGAUD (I), adventurer with a sweeping cloak and delusions of grandeur ("I am a gentleman"), is held in a Marseilles prison. His prominent hook nose comes down to his thick moustache "in a very sinister and cruel manner". Acquittted of murdering his wife but kept in custody because of public hostility, he flees gaol and months later arrives in London and meets Mrs Clennam to make her a proposition which is not detailed.

He disappears and, now calling himself Blandois, attaches himself to the Dorrit family on their European progress. In Venice he poses for Gowan to paint his portrait; Gowan's dog has to be restrained from going for him and is then found poisoned.

On another visit to his mother, Arthur Clennam finds that Rigaud is there again, proposing some undefined business. Arthur protests ineffectually that this visitor is bad company.

Rigaud disappears late that night, apparently without trace. There are handbills out seeking information about him. Clennam is concerned at possible danger and goes in search of him. He also asks Cavaletto for help.

By the time Cavaletto has found him, Arthur has become a Marshalsea prisoner. Cavaletto takes Rigaud to visit him and Rigaud explains that he wanted to put a business proposition to Mrs Clennam and Flintwinch; he writes from Arthur's cell giving her a week to agree to meet.

When the week is up, Rigaud goes to visit Mrs Clennam's warehouse and states his business: it is blackmail – unless Mrs Clennam pays him £2,000 he will reveal to her son that very evening that she has hidden the paper which would have made Little Dorrit rich.

Mrs Clennam is stirred into action, and goes to the Marshalsea to straighten matters out; she is on her way back to the Clennam warehouse with Amy when they see the building explode and go up in flames; Rigaud is killed.

TATTYCORAM (II), Pet Meagles's teenage maid, with "lustrous dark hair and eyes". She is an orphan from the Foundling Hospital given a new opportunity by being taken in by Mr Meagles but she has moods where she violently resents her inferior status and envies the affection her young mistress receives – despite the kind home into which she has been accepted.

When Tattycoram runs off to Miss Wade the distressed Mr Meagles asks Clennam to help try get her back. Miss Wade "just as handsome, just as scornful, just as repressed", takes the girl's side. Meagles warns the girl that Miss Wade's influence "is founded on a passion fiercer than yours".

Months later Tattycoram runs away from Miss Wade and asks to be reinstated in the Meagle household: Pet is now home again so this suits everyone.

WADE, MISS (III), English traveller held in the Marseilles quarantine with the Meagles family and Clennam. She holds herself aloof, "still and scornful" with a cruel mouth.

She comes across Tattycoram angry and weeping, saying how jealous she is of Pet Meagles and how she feels neglected. Calming down, she confesses to Miss Wade that what she has said is lies and that she has been lovingly treated and that she is afraid of herself when she feels her temper rising.

After Rigaud's disappearance Arthur tries to trace him and seeks information from Miss Wade, whom he finds in Calais. She repeats that Rigaud ("mercenary wretch") was merely a courier for her money from Casby. She adds that her manner is cold because she is illegitimate, and not only hates Pet Meagles but also Pet's husband Gowan – to whom she was once close and who had turned away from her to marry another.

She lies to Meagles about not having seen Rigaud subsequently when actually she was given by him the record of Little Dorrit's inheritance. Tattycoram abandons Miss Wade, running away to Mr Meagles, and is reinstated as Pet's maid.

MARTIN CHUZZLEWIT

CHUZZLEWIT, ANTHONY (VIII), is brother to the older Martin; he is aged 80, head of the warehousing firm of Anthony Chuzzlewit and Son, which he runs with Jonas and his elderly clerk Chuffey, is proud that he trained his son to be "sly, cunning and covetous" and also proud that he called his cousin Pecksniff a hypocrite to his face; but he also tells Pecksniff that as the architect's daughter Charity is "of good hard griping stock" she would be a suitable match for Jonas. Anthony has a seizure and dies.

★★★CHUZZLEWIT, JONAS (VIII), Anthony's son is a mean and grasping young man who helps to run his father's warehousing firm and keeps hoping that his father will die soon. From the time he meets the Pecksniffs travelling to London he makes advances to Charity.

Pecksniff is on a visit to the Chuzzlewit warehouse when the old man dies: Jonas tells Pecksniff he is relieved that he is there because it does away with any suspicion about the death, suspicions which will revive later.

He asks Pecksniff what marriage portion he can expect if he marries Charity and is promised £4,000. After Anthony's funeral he accompanies Pecksniff to his home and promptly proposes marriage not to Charity but to Mercy, who calls him a "fright" and slaps his face. Not deterred, Jonas tells Pecksniff that to marry the younger daughter he will want to increase the price to £5,000.

Mercy continues to taunt him and he tells her sourly that when they are married he will repay her a thousand times. He keeps his promise.

Shifty confidence trickster Montague Tigg invites Jonas to join in a bogus insurance company called the Anglo-Bengalee. Jonas thinks that he is making a big coup, never realising he will be not Tigg's partner but his victim, constantly spied on by Tigg's agent Nadgett. He is lavishly entertained to draw him in, comes home drunk and beats up his wife Mercy. Tigg suggests raising more money by drawing in Jonas's relative Pecksniff as well.

Jonas starts feeling out of his depth. He and Mercy, both heavily disguised, try to escape onto a steamer bound for Antwerp, but Tigg – tipped off by the spy Nadgett – gets to him before the boat can sail. Jonas is brought back to the Anglo-Bengalee offices like a "fettered man", the "same imprisoned devil still".

Jonas, trapped, suggests that he and Tigg both go to Pecksniff. On the journey their coach is overturned in a storm and Tigg is thrown to the ground unconscious. Jonas tries to murder Tigg by pulling a frightened horse around so that its hooves will crush his skull; the driver rescues Tigg in time. At the Blue Dragon, a tavern near Pecksniff's home, Jonas and Tigg give Pecksniff a fine dinner and get him to pledge his money – Pecksniff to his delight being named as a full partner in the Anglo-Bengalee.

Jonas returns to London but slips unnoticed out of his quarters to travel back incognito to waylay Tigg after another meeting with Pecksniff; he murders Tigg in a lonely country spot and slips back to his home again unnoticed.

But he *was* noticed by the spy Nadgett – the man who thwarted Jonas's flight to Antwerp.

Nadgett checked on his movements, worked out what had happened and recovered from the Thames at London Bridge the incriminating bundle of clothes Jonas had used as a disguise to double back to the country and kill Tigg. As a police informer, Nadgett accompanies Slyme, another member of the Chuzzlewit clan, to arrest Jonas.

He is not present when Jonas bribes Slyme £100 in cash to give him the opportunity to take the poison which ends his life.

★★★**CHUZZLEWIT, MARTIN (V)**, handsome hero of the story, aged about 21, with a keen dark eye and a quick manner, joins the Pecksniff household as a new architectural pupil. He loves a girl called Mary, who is his grandfather's carer; the love has to be kept secret. He is patronising in his manner to Pecksniff's gentle live-in assistant, Tom Pinch, who is only too glad to be taken notice of.

Pecksniff takes his daughters to London and on his return Martin, who has been working hard on a design for a grammar school, is to his surprise summarily sacked; he does not know that Pecksniff has been put up to this by his grandfather. Angry and humiliated, Martin sets out without a coat to walk to London in the rain, with only a half-guinea from Pinch to tide him over.

He meets Mark Tapley in London; together they decide to go to America. Tapley engineers a meeting with Martin's beloved Mary in St James's Park; they pledge each other's love and Mary spends her savings to give Martin a packet of diamonds to boost his funds; with the characteristic arrogance which he also showed to Pinch he takes it all for granted.

On board ship, Mark makes himself liked by everyone by being helpful as well as cheerful; Martin sulks on his bunk because he does not want to be recognised by anyone in the future as a man who travelled steerage…

He lands in New York and is taken under the wing of Colonel Diver, editor of the *New York Rowdy Journal*, whose thousands of readers could regularly "delight in filth". The colonel's face is a "mixed expression of vulgar cunning and conceit".

Martin and Mark are lured by the crooked entrepreneur General Zephaniah Scadder of the Eden Land Corporation to buy land and take part in a grandiose project where Martin is told he will be able to use his skills to create fine public buildings. Martin pays $150 for a plot of 50 acres in the "thriving city of Eden". Mark is astute enough to see what is happening but Martin is so happy that he promises Mark an equal share in the business, "forever building castles in the air. Forever in his very selfishness, forgetful of all but his teeming hopes … The consciousness of patronising … Mark."

After a long river journey they arrive at their destination and find no city, merely a fetid swamp with their own plot covered with trees. They take shelter in a dilapidated log cabin. Martin weeps; Mark takes charge, arranges the provisions and tells himself that this is a good opportunity to show "a jolly disposition".

Martin develops a severe fever, throughout which Tapley nurses him tirelessly. No sooner has Martin recovered than Tapley falls ill with the same, and it is Martin's turn to devote himself to being helpful. He comes to a self-realisation – that "selfishness was in his breast and must be rooted out".

When they have both recovered they raise what money they can and leave for New York, where Tapley is engaged as cook on the ship that will take them back to England, and Tapley's wages, he explains with generous glee to Martin, will pay for Martin's passage.

They arrive in England and come across a public ceremony where Mr Pecksniff is being feted as a great architect while laying a foundation stone. Building plans are on display; Martin is outraged when he sees that the project was the very grammar school he designed before Pecksniff sacked him.

Martin takes Mark with him to seek out old Martin, to ask him for help in making a fresh start after the American venture. The old man is with Pecksniff, who is at his most offensively patronising; under such influence the old man refuses to help. However, Martin has an opportunity to speak with Mary, still in attendance on his grandfather, and the couple reaffirm their love.

When the grandfather regains his strength and calls all his circle to his chambers in the Temple, Martin is present when Pecksniff is thrashed. Old Martin blesses the nuptials of young Martin and gives his bride Mary Graham a wedding present of earrings and a bracelet.

★★★**CHUZZLEWIT, MARTIN (III)**, brother to Anthony and grandfather to the young Martin, is a strong and vigorous old man with "will of iron and voice of brass". He arrives at the Blue Dragon tavern in Pecksniff's village full of cramps and pain but refuses any assistance. He is accompanied by a "timid and shrinking" dark-haired teenage girl, Mary Graham, who tends him loyally but to whom he is petulant. Mary is the beloved of his grandson and namesake Martin Chuzzlewit.

Pecksniff comes to see him and calls him cousin: the old man retorts that any word of kindred "opens up a calendar of deceit and lying"; his wealth has brought him only revelations of "falsehood, baseness and servility". When the old man retires Pecksniff creeps to his door to hear if anything is being said; he bumps into another eavesdropper, Montague Tigg, who introduces his friend Chevy Slyme.

Slyme claims to be a nephew of old Martin while Pecksniff is a cousin. There is a chaotic family conference in Pecksniff's house during which it is learnt that old Martin and Mary have left the area.

Old Martin comes to visit Pecksniff in London, makes common cause with him and tells him to dismiss his new pupil, i.e. young Martin, for having "betrayed" him by being in love with Mary. Pecksniff obsequiously agrees.

Martin comes to live near Pecksniff, further mends fences with him – and gradually falls into Pecksniff's clutches. His grandson comes to plead for help in getting started after coming back bankrupt from America, but under Pecksniff's total influence old Martin refuses.

Soon after Pecksniff has been sucked into Jonas's scheme, old Martin leaves Pecksniff, comes to London, reveals himself to Tom Pinch as the mysterious landlord of the Temple chambers and is also revealed to have "triumphant purpose"; with all his old strength and vigour, he says that his time with Pecksniff had been to seek out his real character. He calls all his friends around him, and when Pecksniff arrives knocks him to the ground and denounces him as a scoundrel; he says that he had feigned weakness to seek Pecksniff out but had never found any trace of "natural tenderness".

He reveals that he has always been supportive of the love of his grandson Martin for Mary Graham, and sums up, looking kindly on Mary: "The curse of our house has ever been the love of self."

DIVER, COLONEL (XVI), editor of the *New York Rowdy Journal*, which publishes "highly-spiced wares" for readers who "delight in filth". He finds accommodation for Martin on his arrival in New York; Martin finds it was done not out of kindness but for a bribe. The colonel's juvenile assistant is Jefferson Brick, War Correspondent.

GAMP, MRS SARAH ("SAIREY") (XIX), nurse and midwife, is a fat elderly woman always dressed in rusty black gown and bonnet, much the worse for snuff; her face somewhat red and swollen and with "a smell of spirits". She lives in Holborn and always "went to a lying-in or a laying-out with equal zest and relish".

Pecksniff fetches her for professional assistance on the death of Anthony Chuzzlewit and she performs her duties faithfully, as she always does, with liberal libations from the well-fortified contents of her teapot. She befriends Mercy Chuzzlewit, who looks to her for the protection she feels she needs. She still dispenses advice freely with the inspiration of "sundry spirits".

When she is called to look after the Chuzzlewits' old retainer Chuffey, she enlists a colleague Mrs Betsey Prig for assistance for this engagement but her suggestion that Mrs Prig acts as her subordinate greatly offends Mrs Prig as they are both in liquor, and this leads to a quarrel.

Old Martin restored to vigour, he advises Mrs Gamp "of the expediency of a little less liquor and a little more humanity" at which she stages an elaborate walking swoon…

GRAHAM, MARY (III), carer and nurse to old Martin; she is tender and gentle in her manner; he is often rough to her. When Mercy Pecksniff marries and Charity leaves home, Pecksniff looks round for company and proposes marriage to Mary; she rejects him and he threatens to have old Martin disinherit young Martin if she does not yield. She explains to Tom Pinch her situation so fully that Pinch at last sees Pecksniff as he really is and says so loudly. Pecksniff overhears Pinch saying so and sacks him.

Mary remains with old Martin when he is constantly in Pecksniff's company. After young Martin makes a vain approach to his grandfather for help, he and Mary secretly pledge their love again.

When old Martin is restored to strength, he brings the couple together, blesses their union and presents Mary with gifts.

★★★**PECKSNIFF, SETH (II)**, architect in a village near Salisbury, is "full of virtuous precepts", and a "soft and oily manner". "His genius lay in ensnaring parents and guardians and pocketing their premiums" to take in boarders who receive little or no instruction in professional skills. He is a widower always dressed in black with hair standing erect on his forehead; he has "an affable sense of his own excellence". When young trainee John Westlock leaves he denounces Pecksniff for having exploited him for years. He wants to shake hands on departure to let bygones be bygones but Pecksniff spurns him.

Old Martin Chuzzlewit arrives in the vicinity and Pecksniff goes to see his cousin but is met with dislike and contempt. In view of his home being there, various branches of the quarrelsome family converge to see what they can get.

They meet in Pecksniff's parlour, greet his assumption of being head of the clan with derision and taunt him with hypocrisy. Even before the gathering ends in chaos they learn that the old man has left the area anyway.

Pecksniff welcomes his new pupil, the young Martin, and takes his daughters to London, where they put up at the seedy Todgers lodging-house, where Pecksniff passes out after drinking too much.

Old Martin Chuzzlewit mends fences with him and urges him to sack his grandson as one of his pupils; Pecksniff readily agrees.

When Anthony Chuzzlewit dies, Pecksniff goes as part of funeral preparations to fetch from her Holborn home the nurse Mrs Gamp.

At the time of the funeral Jonas asks what he can expect if he marries Charity and Pecksniff says £4,000. When Jonas switches his attentions to Mercy her father accepts the change with equanimity and accepts Jonas's demand for a marriage portion of £5,000.

Jonas marries Mercy and takes her to London. Charity is left alone with her father and in her humiliation at Mercy's marriage is in flat rebellion against him. She decides to leave for London.

Pecksniff, left alone, weighs up his chances and as old Martin is still living nearby asks Mary Graham to marry him. She refuses indignantly; blandly he threatens he will tell old Martin to disinherit young Martin.

He overhears Mary telling Tom Pinch how she had been taken advantage of by Pecksniff and bitterly criticising him and he hears Pinch denouncing him as well, his long-standing illusions having been shattered. With great pretence of sadness, Pecksniff dismisses Pinch.

Young Martin is back in England when he sees Pecksniff basking in general adulation at a public ceremony when laying the foundation stone of a new grammar school; in fact, the plans show (to Martin's disgust) that Pecksniff has appropriated as his own the design Martin drew up in his office.

Pecksniff takes over protection of old Martin and, when young Martin comes seeking help in making a fresh start on his return from America, Pecksniff in his most overbearing manner gets the old grandfather to refuse.

Having conceived the Anglo-Bengalee insurance fraud scheme, Tigg and Jonas conspire together by entertaining Pecksniff at the Blue Dragon and drawing him in completely by making him a partner in the enterprise.

Old Martin Chuzzlewit, back with his vigour restored, visits his chambers in the Temple and with family and friends present awaits Mr Pecksniff's arrival. Pecksniff, seeing his old pupil John Westlock as well as young Martin, Pinch and Mary Graham together, confidently denounces them all as "vermin and bloodsuckers" and seeks to embrace old Martin, who turns and with his stick furiously fells him to the ground, calling him "smooth-tongued, servile crawling knave". He makes it plain that he had feigned weakness to see if Pecksniff showed "the least touch of natural tenderness", but found only "a mean false heart". Pecksniff departs.

He ends his days as a "drunken squalid begging-letter-writing man with a shrewish daughter".

PECKSNIFF, CHARITY ("CHERRY") and MERCY ("MERRY") (II), Pecksniff's daughters, born five years apart, flatter their father, echo his sentiments and beneath fine words always seek spitefully to score points off one another. Charity becomes the object of the attentions of surly rich young businessman Jonas Chuzzlewit, much to the intense mortification of Mercy. After Anthony's death, Jonas comes home with Pecksniff and proposes marriage to Mercy, not Charity.

The latter retires to her room with "an hysterical infection"; the younger daughter slaps Jonas's face and says that she "might hate and tease you all my life". Soon, in front of others, Mercy "rejoiced in the triumph of her conquest". She "probed and lanced the rankling disappointment of her sister", while Charity suffers "unspeakable jealousy and hatred".

Mercy continuously mocks and taunts Jonas and keeps putting off the wedding day. Old Martin warns her to be careful about her attitude and about marrying at all, because Jonas will get his own back once they are married – which is what Jonas keeps telling her.

He marries Mercy, and as soon as they are are home in London together he turns on her. She is soon "fallen, humbled, broken". He assaults her when he comes back drunk from a night out after sealing the Anglo-Bengalee business deal with Tigg.

Charity, left alone with her father and with "a sense of slight and injury", is in flat rebellion against him and proposes that she go to London. He puts on a false show of reluctance but readily agrees.

Charity is put up at the lodging-house, where the owner Mrs Todgers always panders to her caprices.

Wherever she goes in London, Charity "sticks pretty close to the vinegar bottle" in her attitudes, but in the lodging-house meets "the youngest lodger", the gentle Augustus Moddle, whom she overwhelms as her "intended" and makes this plain to all around her; Moddle seems increasingly hapless in her grasp.

Mercy is forced to accompany Jonas on an attempted flight to Antwerp as his business involvement becomes more complex and is brought back to London in a distressed state. Back at home, she confesses: "You promised me before we married that you would break my spirit – and you have done so."

Jonas is murdered; old Martin Chuzzlewit provides the humbled Mercy with help to start a new life.

Charity pursues Mr Moddle; on the wedding day, already in her bridal finery, she gets a note from him that he is sailing for Australia. Shrewish as ever, she returns to share existence with her bankrupt father.

PINCH, TOM (II), aged 35, gentle, ungainly, short-sighted, prematurely bald; always patient, courteous; live-in assistant to Pecksniff. His friend John Westlock assesses him: "Pecksniff trades on your nature ... timid and distrustful of yourself, and trustful ... of him who least deserves it". Organist in the local church; his employer gains standing from Pinch's good works.

On young Martin's dismissal, he slips him a half-guinea he could himself ill afford.

After Martin has been long silent in America, Tom meets Mary Graham and reports the lack of news. Mary tells him that Pecksniff had tried to take advantage of her by proposing marriage and denounces him so stoutly that Tom, who has long been secretly but deeply in love with Mary, is finally robbed of his illusion and criticises him, too. Pecksniff overhears their conversation and after returning home, with a façade of deep sorrow at Tom's "betrayal", dismisses him.

Tom's departure from the village is mourned by everyone except Pecksniff; the sympathetic Blue Dragon licensee Mrs Lupin slips him £5 to help things along.

Tom reaches London and rescues his sister Ruth, a pretty little woman but mild like her brother, from her unhappy position as governess to a nouveau-riche family and with his newfound self-confidence soundly berates her employer before taking her away.

Tom and Ruth set up home in Islington very happily. Tom is found a job at £100 a year as a librarian to an unknown tenant of chaotic chambers in the Temple, which gives him lots of tidying up to do, again very happily. Ruth revels in her domestic duties.

There is a strange footstep on the stairs of the Temple chambers where Tom has been organising the library for his mysterious landlord. It is the landlord who appears – old Martin, with "resolute face, watchful eye and vigorous hand". Martin says that all his time with Pecksniff was just to test out his character and his schemes.

Pecksniff is denounced and discarded. Ruth Pinch marries her brother's friend John Westlock and has a wedding gift of a bracelet and earrings from old Martin. Tom will live with the couple, who will have a daughter; Tom will continue his career as organist.

SLYME, CHEVY (IV), a short man, "maudlin, insolent and beggarly" with sharp features and red whiskers, is a nephew of old Martin Chuzzlewit (while Pecksniff is a cousin). Pecksniff is caught eavesdropping at the old man's door to see what he can find out, finds Tigg doing the same and is then led to Tigg's friend Slyme, who informs Pecksniff that various branches of the Chuzzlewit family are to meet that day to reach the old man to see what *they* can find out. Slyme joins the party, which ends in squabbles.

In the final chapters, Slyme returns as a police officer to arrest Jonas for Tigg's murder. Jonas, left alone with Slyme, bribes him with £100 to be left alone and Jonas takes poison.

***TAPLEY, MARK (V)**, mid-twenties, good-humoured, comical fellow, blue eyes, merry manner, irrepressibly buoyant. He is fond of Mrs Lupin, buxom landlady of the Blue Dragon, where he works, but leaves the job to try his fortune in London, where he will, by his own often-proclaimed credo, seek to be jolly, particularly in adverse circumstances.

He meets young Martin after the latter's departure from Pecksniff's, offers his services "as a nat'ral born servant" free of charge to help carry out Martin's intention of travelling to the United States, "for that's the place for me to be jolly in".

When they arrive at the inland site where Martin is to practise as an architect they find it a desolate swamp. This is too much for Martin, who breaks down; Mark take charge and puts things in order because "now's your time to come out strong!"

He nurses Martin through an attack of fever and when he himself falls ill Martin nurses him in return.

Both recovered, they raise what resources they can and quit Eden. In New York they find that the ship that will take them back to England is short of a cook. Mark is hired to do the job, and what he earns will pay for Martin to travel as a passenger.

When old Martin returns to strength and vigour and solves the problems of young Martin and everyone else, Mark promises to marry the jolly Blue Dragon landlady Mrs Lupin and to rename her inn the Jolly Tapley.

TIGG, MONTAGUE (IV), evil countenance, dirty and jaunty, shaggy moustache, confidant and "adopted brother" to Chevy Slyme, catches Pecksniff eavesdropping on old Chuzzlewit, introduces Pecksniff to Slyme as another relative and tries to touch Pecksniff for a small loan – without success.

He sets up in London a company called the Anglo-Bengalee Disinterested Loan and Life Assurance Company to attract and fleece investors, and wines and dines Jonas Chuzzlewit, who seeks to profit by the company, not aware that Tigg is making him his dupe.

Tigg spurs Jonas to expand their scheme by entrapping Pecksniff; Jonas feels trapped himself and seeks to escape to Antwerp but is found just in time by his fellow director. He now himself proposes that he and Tigg should go to Pecksniff together.

Jonas tries to murder Tigg when their coach overturns but Tigg survives; Jonas and Tigg draw Pecksniff into their scheme; having sealed the deal Jonas waylays Tigg in a lonely spot and murders him.

WESTLOCK, JOHN (II), Pecksniff's trainee at the start of the story, departs pointing out to Pecksniff how he has been exploited; goes to London and comes into money; remains friends with Pinch and puts him up when Tom leaves Pecksniff; marries Tom's sister Ruth; he and Ruth will have a daughter.

THE MYSTERY OF EDWIN DROOD

The only novel Dickens left unfinished, its riddles unresolved.

BUD, ROSA (III), pretty orphan, but "spoilt, amiable and giddy". She is a student at Miss Twinkleton's seminary in the cathedral city of Cloisterham, intended to be married to Edwin Drood when he comes of age – but they are ill at ease together when they meet.

On Christmas Eve, Rosa and Edwin decide amicably to end the engagement. A few hours later Edwin vanishes.

Rosa's music teacher, John Jasper, choirmaster in the cathedral whose dour manner has always unsettled her, comes to her the summer after Edwin's disappearance and confesses his "mad love" for her; she faints out of terror, wondering if Jasper got Edwin out of the way so he could pursue her himself. She flees to London, where her guardian finds her a home.

CRISPARKLE, REV. SEPTIMUS (II), aged 35, canon in Cloisterham cathedral, "good-natured, contented and boy-like" bachelor who lives with his mother, takes charge of a new arrival from Ceylon, young Neville Landless, and is alarmed when on their first meeting Neville speaks of someone he might have been provoked to murder. Neville comes back the first night drunk and furious after a clash with Edwin Drood in Jasper's lodgings. Crisparkle urges reconciliation. After Edwin's disappearance on Christmas Eve, suspicions against Neville mount and he leaves Crisparkle's charge.

DATCHERY, DICK (XVIII), white-haired, describing himself as a single buffer, comes to stay at Cloisterham and methodically pursues the Drood case – the significance undisclosed.

★★★**DROOD, EDWIN (II)**, little more than a boy, amiable, light-hearted. He is preparing in London to be an engineer and when he is of age he will go to work in Egypt. His father and Rosa Bud's father agreed before they died that their children should marry.

Edwin comes to Cloisterham to stay with his guardian John Jasper and calls at the seminary where Rosa is a student; he takes her for a walk but they are mutually ill at ease. Jasper entertains him and Neville in his lodgings. Flushed with drink, Neville is irritated at Edwin's self-satisfied manner and tells him his easy life should have had a few knocks because he has become just a boaster. Edwin retorts: "You are no judge of white men." In a violent argument Jasper keeps the two youths apart and Neville leaves in a rage.

Edwin promises Jasper that when he returns from London at Christmas he will make up with Neville. On Christmas Eve he comes to stay with his guardian; he meets Rosa and they agree amicably to cancel the engagement.

That evening he and Neville meet in Jasper's rooms, after which they go to the river near the town to look at an exceptional storm that is blowing. Neville then sets off for a walking tour.

Edwin vanishes. Despite extensive searches in the river and the surrounding area he is not seen again. His watch and a shirt-pin are recovered from Cloisterham Weir.

★★★**JASPER, JOHN (I)**, dark man, aged about 26, lustrous black hair and whiskers, voice deep and good, a fine singer but with a sombre manner. He is a respected choirmaster at Cloisterham cathedral; he is also an opium addict. He lives alone and has "devoted affection" for his young nephew, Edwin Drood, to whom he is guardian.

Entertaining Edwin and the newly arrived Neville Landless with powerful mulled wine in his lodgings, there is an argument, tempers flare and he has to restrain the drunken Neville from assaulting Edwin. On Crisparkle's initiative he arranges that on Christmas Eve the two young men will meet again at Jasper's to make up. They leave their host late that evening.

The next day Jasper hears that Edwin has vanished and is then told by Rosa's guardian that the engagement was terminated; the news makes Jasper shriek and collapse in a swoon.

Having recovered, he writes in his diary that he is convinced Edwin has been murdered and that he will never stop his search for the murderer. It becomes public knowledge that he pursues this aim; he concentrates on seeking to pin down Neville.

Six months later he confesses to Rosa that he loves her and "would pursue her to the death". Terrified, she runs away. He comes to London, visits the opium den again and returns to Cloisterham where he is secretly followed by the drug dealer – the significance of which is not disclosed.

LANDLESS, HELENA (VI), "lustrous gypsy face", "womanly and handsome", a person with resolution and power, dark fiery eyes, black hair and dark skin" like her twin brother, makes friends with Rosa at the seminary. She believes suspicions of her brother are unfounded.

★★★LANDLESS, NEVILLE (VI), "unusually handsome lithe young fellow", dark and rich in colour, with "air of a hunter", fierce of look, half-shy and half-defiant. He and his sister grew up in Ceylon with a harsh stepfather.

He says it is as well the stepfather "died when he did, or I might have killed him". He tells this to Crisparkle, with whom he is to live to further his education. Crisparkle fears his is "a mis-shapen mind".

When Neville meets Edwin he tells the younger man that he has had too easy a life. Resentment flares, the more when Edwin says: "You are no judge of white men." Neville, furious at this reference to his dark skin, smashes his glass in the fireplace, leaves and goes home, telling Crisparkle that Drood had heated his "tigerish blood". When Crisparkle suggests that Neville apologises, he refuses because he is still "sensible of inexpressable affront", and that while he feels Edwin is quite unworthy of Rosa he (Neville) loves her "so very much I cannot bear her being treated with conceit or indifference". He agrees to be reconciled with Edwin at Jasper's rooms on Christmas Eve, after which Neville was to set off on an extensive walking tour because – as he tells his sister – he wants to stay out of the way because of his "inflammable reputation", but first the two youths set off together for the river to admire a storm.

Neville then sets off on the tour just as he had planned, but is brought back by force the next day and accused because Edwin is missing. There is blood on his clothes, which Neville claims was caused when he fought the men coming to bring him back to Cloisterham. He claims that Edwin was heading back to Jasper's rooms when he vanished. Neville is ordered to remain with Crisparkle but prejudice against him mounts – Cloisterham's mayor Sapsea remarks on his "un-English complexion" – and he leaves the town. The loyal Crisparkle sets him up as a law student in London, a study at which he makes quiet progress, not knowing that Jasper is still seeking to trap him.

NICHOLAS NICKLEBY

BRAY, MADELINE (XLVI), "fresh, lovely, bewitching and not nineteen", lives with her bullying wastrel invalid father Walter; Nicholas is sent to her as the Cheerybles' go-between to pass badly-needed money on the pretext of buying her pictures.

Bray is heavily in debt both to Ralph Nickleby and to an old money-lender friend Arthur Gride; a deal is done whereby the debt is written off if Walter sells his daughter in marriage to the seedy septuagenarian Gride, Madeline having been persuaded she must submit out of loyalty to her father.

Ralph Nickleby's clerk Noggs comes to know of this from overhearing Ralph and warns Nicholas; Nicholas goes to Madeline and begs her at least to wait, but she says that she has to go ahead with it because it will give her father comfortable circumstances in his last years. Nicholas goes to Gride's mean lodgings and desperately offers to pay him off; Gride sends him away.

On the wedding morning, Gride and Ralph are first to arrive at Madeline's home; Nicholas arrives with Kate, denounces both men and says he will take Madeline away. Upstairs a thud is heard – Bray has fallen down dead. Nicholas takes Madeline to safety. A stolen will recovered from Gride's rooms leaves her £12,000. She marries Nicholas.

BROWDIE, JOHN (IX), tall, jovial, young Yorkshireman, engaged to marry the friend of Fanny Squeers, thereby incurring Fanny's envy because the friend will soon have a husband, and spite because Fanny wanted him herself.

Browdie and his Tilda come to a tea party at Dotheboys where Fanny hoped to show off Nicholas likewise as a suitor and is humiliated at her failure when he takes no notice.

When Nicholas hits the road penniless and hopeless after thrashing Squeers, the kindly Browdie lends him a sovereign to help him on his way; when Browdie is on his honeymoon in London he meets Squeers exulting in the recapture of Smike; Browdie slips away and surreptitiuously frees him.

He meets Squeers again and denounces him for a rascal; he also prevents Snawley from taking Smike away from the Nicklebys.

CHEERYBLE, CHARLES and EDWIN (NED) (XXXV), benevolent and public-spirited twin brothers who set up in business in the City over 40 years ago and have a prosperous warehouse in a square behind Threadneedle Street.

Charles, "a sturdy fellow in broad-skirted blue coat" and an "honest, merry, happy eye", meets Nicholas by chance when Nicholas is looking for a job in an agency window (after having cut short his career as a schoolmaster and as an actor), takes him home to meet brother Ned, likewise a cheerful kindly man; they give Nicholas a job in their counting-house and set the Nickleby family up for a new life with a cottage in Bow.

CRUMMLES, NINETTA (XXIII), the "infant phenomenon", the dancer in her father's theatre group, also plays straight roles as required. He gives her age as 10 but she looks older "as she had been kept up late every night and put upon an unlimited diet of gin-and-water from infancy to prevent her growing tall".

CRUMMLES, VINCENT (XXII), a large heavy man with a hoarse voice and black hair cut short so he can wear wigs for a variety of roles in his travelling group of strolling players. He meets Nicholas and Smike when on their way to Portsmouth and offers them jobs. He is delighted with the success Nicholas has both as an actor and as a scriptwriter and gives him an emotional send-off when his star leaves for London. Eventually the family emigrate to the United States.

KNAG, MISS (X), forewoman in Mantalini showroom; unkind to Kate Nickleby; takes over when Alfred Mantalini bankrupts the firm.

MANTALINI, MADAME (X), milliner and dressmaker with premises in Cavendish Square employing 20 young women under forewoman Miss Knag. Nicholas's young sister Kate Nickleby is engaged to work at a salary of between five and seven shillings a week. Madame had married a flirtatious and spendthrift husband called Alfred Muntel; the Italianised name would be better for trade.

His spending bankrups the firm; the bailiffs move in and the business is taken over by Miss Knag. Mantalini fakes a suicide attempt in an attempt to win his wife back but without success. The husband ends up as a labourer turning a mangle in a laundry.

★★★NICKLEBY, KATE (III), aged about 17, "slight but very beautiful", Nicholas's sister is given a job as a milliner by Madame Mantalini. She falls foul of the overbearing forewoman Miss Knag when a customer in the showroom prefers to be attended by the prettier and much younger Kate.

Ralph Nickleby invites Kate to a dinner of men who he intends to ensnare in his business deals, particularly Sir Mulberry Hawk and his weak-minded friend Lord Frederick Verisopht.

Kate goes home in a distressed state, so affected by the evening that she has to stay away from work for three days. When she goes back she finds that the bailiffs are taking over the Mantalini business, which has gone bankrupt.

As she is now jobless, Kate answers an advertisement and is taken on as lady's companion by Mrs Julia Wititterly, a hypochondriac "bursting with pride and arrogance" living in Cadogan Place off Sloane Square.

Kate is relentlessly pursued by Hawk and Lord Frederick, and at last goes to her uncle for protection but in vain. Nicholas comes to London to rescue her and takes her away from Mrs Witilterly. Kate first moves back to her friend the portrait painter Miss La Creevy, and when Nicholas lands his job with the Cheeryble brothers moves to the cottage in Bow with mother, brother and Smike.

She accompanies Nicholas to the Brays' home on the morning before the scheduled marriage of Gride and Madeline and helps Nicholas take Madeline away.

Kate falls in love with the Cheeryble brothers' handsome nephew Frank and marries him.

★★★**NICKLEBY, NICHOLAS (III)**, the hero, aged 18, with "open, handsome and ingenuous face, of good family and well-educated", is left penniless by his late father's bad investments. He has to find a job and is urged by his uncle Ralph to apply to become a schoolteacher at Dotheboys Hall in Yorkshire at a salary of £5 a year.

He meets the head of Dotheboys, Wackford Squeers, and they journey north with a number of unhappy and starved-looking new pupils. When the coach overturns in the snow Nicholas wins praise by saving the day.

On Nicholas's first morning he sees the pupils given brimstone and treacle by Squeers because, as Squeers says, "it spoils their appetites and is cheaper than breakfast and dinner". He sees Squeers steal clothes and money sent to the boys and conduct a class where he beats and bullies the pupils.

Nicholas finds a lonely friend in the mentally backward assistant Smike and after a day in the midst of cold misery feels "depressed and self-degraded".

When Squeers's daughter Fanny invites to him to tea in the hope of making a conquest and gets no response she becomes bitter and sees to it that general resentment is taken out not only on Nicholas but also on the defenceless Smike, subjected by the family to "stripes and blows morning noon and night". As Nicholas is always kind, Smike weeps as he says, "but for you I should die".

Smike runs away and is brought back by Squeers and his wife; Nicholas unavailingly pleads for Smike; the drunken and enraged Squeers starts a vicious beating. Nicholas urges him to stop and Squeers spits at him and strikes him. Nicholas takes the stick from him and beats Squeers to the ground.

He collects his belongings and his money – some four shillings in all – and starts on the road to London. The friendly Yorkshireman John Browdie lends him a sovereign; he sleeps in a cottage the first night and next day finds that Smike has followed him and begs to join him.

Together they continue their journey south and Newman Noggs puts them up. Nicholas, desperate to earn money where he can, is engaged by Noggs's neighbours the Kenwigs family to teach French to their four little daughters at a salary of five shillings a week – a job he holds only briefly.

He goes to see his mother and sister and finds his uncle Ralph already denouncing him. Kate is in tears and defends her brother: Nicholas recounts why he left Dotheboys. Ralph says he withdraws all assistance to his nephew and would do nothing "to save him from the loftiest gallows in all Europe".

Nicholas goes home disconsolate, determined to leave London. Smike offers to go his own way but Nicholas says: "The word which separates us shall never be said by me, for you are my only comfort and stay."

Nearing Portsmouth they meet Vincent Crummles, owner of a group of strolling players, who offers them both a job. Nicholas writes a melodrama for the troupe and acts in it: the show is an "extraordinary success" and he gets a bonus of 30 shillings. He continues to shine in various parts and has a benefit night which nets him £20.

Ralph's clerk Newman Noggs tells him to come back to London

at once because of Kate's situation and in a hotel he hears two men speaking disparagingly about "little Kate Nickleby" and indulge in "licentious jesting". Nicholas confronts Mulberry Hawk and beats him but he gets away.

Nicholas immediately takes Kate away from Mrs Wititterly and his mother from the lodgings provided by Ralph. He houses them with his friend the portrait painter Miss La Creevy and sends a note to Ralph denouncing him.

Going to an agency to seek a new job, he encounters by chance Charles Cheeryble and also meets his brother Ned; he is engaged in their warehouse at £120 a year and is granted a cottage by the Cheerybles in Bow for him, his mother, sister and Smike.

Nicholas acts as a go-beween to give funds from the Cheerybles to young and beautiful Madeline Bray in the form of commissions for small artworks. He falls in love with her and is appalled when he hears she is to marry the elderly moneylender Grice: she is being sold at the price of her father's debts being cancelled.

He pleads in vain with her at least to delay the ceremony but she says she is bound in honour to ease her father's last years. He also pleads with Grice, who sends him away.

On the wedding morning he takes Kate with him to prevent the ceremony. Madeline's father drops dead, and Nicholas carries Madeline in his arms to safety.

He and Madeline are married. With his wife's money he buys a partnership: the firm becomes Cheeryble and Nickleby.

★★★**NICKLEBY, RALPH (I)**, uncle of Nicholas Nickleby, set out from an early age to pursue money-making by usury and other means; lives in a spacious house in Golden Square where he keeps himself to himself. He has "a cold restless eye which seemed to tell of cunning".

Having found lowly jobs for his nephew Nicholas and his niece Kate he moves Kate and her mother to "a gloomy, dingy house" he owns in Thames Street fronting wharves on the river.

He hears from Dotheboys Hall a slanted account of the circumstances of Nicholas's departure. He goes to denounce his nephew with Mrs Nickleby and Kate – and Nicholas arrives in time to refute his charges. Ralph says he will never render further help.

Ralph invites Kate to dinner to draw rich businessmen into his schemes: he has already netted £2,000 from Lord Frederick Verisopht and will use Kate as a bait to draw him and others in still further. After being pursued for a fortnight Kate goes to her uncle in desperation but he refuses to help.

A critical note from Nicholas accusing him fills him even more with "deadly hatred" for Nicholas; when Squeers comes to London they plot against him, pick up Snawley – the man who acts as London agent for Squeers – and go the Nicklebys, where Snawley falsely claims paternity of Smike and seeks to take him away; the big-built Browdie knocks Squeers sideways and Squeers, Ralph and Snawley leave empty-handed.

Nicholas and Kate prevent Gride's wedding; to obtain revenge Ralph sets up Squeers to trace Gride's papers, which have been purloined, and pledges him £100 in gold if he succeeds; the papers would revive his fortune.

Through the Cheeryble brothers Ralph hears that Smike was his own son. Squeers and Newman Noggs turn against him; with the real will brought to light and the money gone, Ralph reflects on all he has lost and hangs himself.

NICKLEBY, MRS (I), mother of Nicholas and Kate Nickleby and wife of Nicholas Nickleby the elder, never "in the possession of a very clear understanding", urged her husband to speculate with the family money, with results that he died in penury. Poverty has not increased her common sense and she always gives wrong advice.

NOGGS, NEWMAN (II), clerk to Ralph Nickleby, who he serves "for rather less than the usual wages of a boy of thirteen"; his taciturn manner suits an office where much secretive business is done. Kind-hearted, he sends Nicholas a secret note offering him shelter if he falls on hard times, an offer taken up after Nicholas has beaten up Squeers and, with Smike in tow, returns to London.

He overhears Ralph scheming with Gride to sell Kate into marriage and warns Nicholas. Also finding that Squeers has been set up by Ralph to recover Gride's stolen deed box, he reaches Squeers just in time to rescue a document about Madeline's assets. With the plot foiled and Ralph dead, Newman is given shelter with the Nicklebys and enjoys playing with the children of Nicholas and Madeline.

★★★**SMIKE (VII)**, aged nineteen, a tall, lean boy, unpaid assistant at Dotheboys; he is lame and "a poor, half-witted creature" still wearing child's clothing and boots "too patched and tattered for a beggar". Nicholas soon befriends and helps him and he weeps with gratitude. When he runs away, Squeers and his wife go searching for him and bring him back looking starved, "more dead than alive".

In front of the entire school, Squeers, who is not only furious but drunk, starts a sadistic beating. Nicholas protests and when Squeers strikes him he snatches the stick back and beats him senseless.

Hurriedly he leaves Dotheboys and heads south; next morning he finds Smike has followed him and begs to be allowed to accompany him. Together they journey to London and are put up by Noggs.

When Nicholas is again in difficulties, Smike offers to leave him to ease his situation; Nicholas swears he will never abandon Smike.

Nicholas is offered a job in the Crummles theatre group and takes Smike in with him; he takes great pains to rehearse Smike successfully for a role in one of the shows. Smike goes back to London with him and when Nicholas gets a post with the Cheeryble brothers Smike moves into the cottage in Bow with the Nicklebys.

Out one evening, he is confronted by Squeers and his son; they kidnap him with the intention of taking him back to Dotheboys.

Squeers's old Yorkshire acquaintance John Browdie, in London on his honeymoon, hears about Smike from Squeers and quietly leaves and sets Smike free.

Smike, happy with the Nicklebys, is appalled when Ralph, Squeers and Squeers's agent Snawley come to the cottage and Snawley claims fictitious paternity of Smike. With Browdie to protect him, the attempt to abduct Smike and return him to Dotheboys fails, but the call is a great shock to Smike and his health begins to decline.

He is taken to Devon in the hope of curing his consumption. He weakens even further, reveals that he has always secretly loved Kate – and dies. After his death it is revealed that Ralph Nickleby was his father.

★★★SQUEERS, WACKFORD (IV), in his early fifties, "one eye, wrinkled face, harsh voice, coarse manner, ill-fitting clothes", is head of Dotheboys Hall in Yorkshire, which boards boys who are abandoned, foundlings or illegitimate. He meets Nicholas in London, engages him as "first assistant master" (although there are no others) and bullies and punches a timid little boy who has just been recruited as a new pupil.

Squeers tells Nicholas that his policy is "to get as much out of the boys as possible": he charges 20 guineas per annum per pupil and systematically robs the boys of gifts or money sent to them.

Squeers, Nicholas and a number of new boys travel north. When the coach overturns in the severe wintry weather Nicholas saves the horses and wins praise for presence of mind.

On the first morning Squeers and Nicholas go to the bare, cold schoolroom with a crowd of boys with "pale haggard faces, lank and bony figures, children with the countenances of old men, deformities with irons upon their limbs, boys of stunted growth … little faces darkened with the scowl of sullen, dogged suffering". In January the school, a single-storey building with outhouses, is cold and unheated.

Mrs Squeers, "a large raw-boned woman with dirty nightcap

and hoarse voice", dispenses brimstone and treacle as it will spoil the children's appetites and they will eat less.

Squeers starts a lesson and spells "window" as w-i-n-d-e-r, and a knowledge of botany is b-o-t-t-i-n-e-y.

Fanny Squeers, very much a spinster daughter, has a young woman friend who constantly flaunts her fiancé, so Fanny is anxious to show off an admirer too and invites Nicholas to tea to make an impression; he in all innocence fails to act the part, creating spiteful resentment; when he is accosted again he makes it plain that he wants "one day to turn my back on this accursed place".

Fanny, of "a constitutionally vicious temper", sets the family against Nicholas. Smike is subjected to even more blows and taunts than before.

When Smike runs away, Mr and Mrs Squeers go searching and bring him back and Squeers begins a beating at which Nicholas protests. Squeers hits out at Nicholas, who snatches the stick and soundly beats Squeers until he "lay at his full length upon the ground, stunned and motionless". Nicholas leaves.

Time passes. Squeers comes to London with his son Wackford and by chance meet Smike, whom they seize and imprison, taunting with blows and abuse and triumphantly speaking of bringing him back to Dotheboys. Squeers is thwarted: they also meet in London their old Yorskhire acquaintance John Browdie, who pretends to sympathise with Squeers but secretly steals out and sets Smike free.

When Squeers visits London again, the deeds box of Ralph's money-lending friend Grice is stolen by his housekeeper on the day Grice was to be married; it contains papers the loss of which will ruin both him and Ralph. Ralph sets Squeers to trace the old housekeeper; he tricks her into handing it over.

As Squeers is about to pocket a parchment registering Madeline Bray as heir to a fortune (by which he could recover his own), Newman Noggs, who has stolen into the room behind him, knocks him senseless. He is arrested and sentenced to seven years' transportation for being in possession of a stolen will.

When the news reaches Dothebys the school breaks up: pupils rebel with joy, duck young Wackford in a bowl of the hated gruel and disperse.

VERISOPHT, LORD FREDERICK, (XIX), feeble-minded young aristocrat whom Ralph Nickleby seeks to draw into his financial web; Kate Nickleby is appalled by his behaviour at a business dinner and flees. He has already yielded Ralph a profit of £2,000 and begs Ralph for the address of this "deyv'lish fine girl".

Nicholas is furious when he overhears Lord Frederick and his friend Hawk in a London hotel discussing "little Kate Nickleby" in unmistakeable terms and assaults Hawk.

Hawk is confined to bed for weeks and on a visit from Ralph threatens extravagant revenge on Nicholas. Lord Frederick overhears this, tells Hawk and Ralph that Kate is a virtuous girl and that Nicholas was right in acting as he did: "I only wish that anyone of us came out of this matter half as well as he does". And he walks out.

Hawk goes abroad to nurse his injury and when back in England again threatens revenge on Nicholas. On a drunken outing Lord Frederick strikes him in protest. A duel is called for; Hawk shoots Lord Frederick dead and flees abroad. Years later he dies in prison.

THE OLD CURIOSITY SHOP

***BRASS, SAMPSON (XII)**, lawyer in the Bevis Marks quarter of London, "a rather doubtful character" with a repulsive smile, comes to help the dwarf Quilp evict the Old Curiosity Shop's elderly owner and his granddaughter Nell from their property.

Always with Brass in his business is his sister Sally, a mean-spirited spinster much tougher than her brother. The servile Brass takes in Richard Swiveller as a clerk under pressure from Quilp, and with Quilp frames Kit Nubbles for theft. Cornered by the Single Gentleman and his lawyer, Brass signs a confession to release Kit and denounces Quilp for having never treated "me otherwise than as a dog". Brass is condemned to prison and the treadmill.

JARLEY, MRS (XXVI), genial owner of a travelling waxworks show, gives Nell a job as presenter of the exhibits, a job at which she excels.

*** **LITTLE NELL (I)**, and her ***GRANDFATHER**, their wanderings after fleeing from the curiosity shop they have so long owned give their part of the narrative a picaresque quality.

Nell (family name Trent) is nearly 14, small and delicate frame, light brown hair, clear blue eyes, a "pretty little girl", "fresh from God". She is an orphan living with her grandfather, to whom she is close. She has intense loyalty but despite her youth also the capacity to think for both of them – she has to.

The grandfather (never named) is a worn-out widower who

deals in curiosities; he is possessively fond of his Nellie. He has a secret weakness which soon emerges – he is a gambling addict.

He has played away his shop and all assets and is heavily in debt to the dwarf Quilp, who has lent him money to fund his habit. A serious illness has left him with dementia, "with fears of being led away".

Quilp moves into the shop to secure his assets and Nellie decides she and the old man should quit before they are evicted. They head out of London first west and then north; it is June and they are helped by almost constant good weather.

They have a number of encounters: a troupe of dancing dogs; stilt walkers; a shady bickering pair of Punch and Judy men; a gentle schoolmaster whose much-loved little pupil dies while they are there; Mrs Jarley, friendly boss of a travelling waxworks collection who employs Nell as master of ceremonies – at which she is a great success.

The grandfather comes across a card school and at once his old weakness comes back. He loses all their money, steals from Nell and presses her constantly for more still. She overhears the card sharps urging the old man to rob Mrs Jarley. Nell judges it best to flee the town.

Times are hard: her strength is fading and "thoughtful care already mingled with the winning grace and loveliness of youth". They are unaware that in London the Single Gentleman has arrived and is seeking to restore them to security just as Quilp is seeking to rob them.

Nell and grandfather meet again the kindly schoolmaster, who is on his way to a new job near the Welsh border and takes them with him to a congenial village.

He finds them a home next to his and they feel safe and happy, but the old man takes on more housework chores as he sees that Nell is slowly fading. When the Single Gentleman reaches their home he is too late: Nell has died. The grandfather cannot bear to leave and sits by her grave daily until, months later, he is found dead.

NUBBLES, KIT (I), snub-nosed and awkward but kind-hearted neighbourhood boy, who keeps a watch on lonely Nellie when her grandfather is out gambling and offers her a home when they face eviction from their shop – but Nell prefers to get away from Quilp.

Kit is befriended by "very quiet regular folks", Mr and Mrs Garland, who give him a job at £6 a year at their home in Finchley. They and Kit are in frequent contact with the Single Gentleman in seeking Nell and the old man; to get Kit away from the Garlands, Quilp and Brass set him up as a thief and have him sent to gaol.

When the plot is discovered Kit is set free and joins the Single Gentleman on his journey north to find the lost couple. He had taken with him the caged bird which Nell had in the curiosity shop days and hoped to restore it to her – but too late.

Kit marries sweetheart Barbara and has a large family.

*** QUILP, DANIEL (III), misshapen middle-aged man with large head and shoulders and short legs, harsh features, dirty and unkempt; money-lender and rent-collector involved in shady deals. When the grandfather cannot repay the money he owes, the dwarf seizes and closes the curiosity shop while the old man is out of action with a fever, and moves in himself with his friend and lawyer Brass.

When Nell and the grandfather flee he is anxious to trace them because he believes they have money; when he hears they have gone north he goes in search but finds he has missed them.

Back in London Kit calls him "you little monster" and Quilp has his revenge: he gets Kit gaoled on a trumped-up charge of theft. When the matter is discovered, authority comes to fetch him in his riverside den; seeking to escape in thick fog Quilp falls into the Thames and is swept to his death by the tide.

***SINGLE GENTLEMAN (XXXIV), bald middle-aged well-spoken man arrives in London nameless and unannounced at Brass's office and rents lodgings there because he knew Brass was in at the seizure of the curiosity shop – and he soon makes it plain his aim is to find its former owner. After information from the Punch and Judy men who had met Nell and the grandfather on their journey, he heads north but finds from Mrs Jarley the trail has gone cold. He meets Quilp, who is on the same quest, and angrily says that through the dwarf the old man was "reduced to sudden beggary". He pursues his search and eventually hears where the pair are and that the young girl has been "weak and ailing", so he wastes no time to go north, taking with him Mr Garland and the newly-released Kit, but Nell has just died. The Single Gentleman reveals that he is the grandfather's estranged brother, returned from a long stay abroad "with honourable wealth enough".

SWIVELLER, RICHARD (II), cheerful, easily led, hard-drinking young man. Quilp ropes him in to help find the old man and get the imaginary fortune – with the promise that he might marry Nell.

Quilp arranges for him to become clerk to lawyer Sampson Brass: to the dwarf he is useful as a spy as long as the Single Gentleman lives in Brass's lodgings because "he tells, in his cups, all that he sees and hears". Richard is witness to Kit's entrapment and pays for the boy to have a daily pint of porter in his cell.

Swiveller falls seriously ill but recovers; an aunt leaves him £150 a year. He pays for the schooling of the little servant who tended him tirelessly when he was ill – and when she is 19 he marries her.

OLIVER TWIST

***BROWNLOW, Mr (X)**, "respectable-looking personage with powered hair and gold spectacles", is browsing in a bookshop when the pickpocket Artful Dodger relieves him of his pocket handkerchief. The horrified Oliver Twist sees this, panics and runs. He is seized.

In court Mr Brownlow tells Fang the magistrate he is convinced of Oliver's innocence and takes him home. On his first errand for Brownlow, Oliver is kidnapped by Nancy. After Oliver is recovered and his affairs are settled Brownlow adopts Oliver: in a way a link has been completed, for many years ago Mr Brownlow would have married the young sister of Oliver's father had she not died.

BUMBLE, MR (II), fat choleric and pompous beadle in cocked hat, bullies the slightly-built Oliver.

CLAYPOLE, NOAH (V), evil-tempered burly long-legged teenage apprentice at Sowerberry funeral parlour, bullies and taunts Oliver. When he insults the memory of Oliver's mother the smaller boy knocks him down. Noah gets Oliver thrashed; Oliver runs away. Much later, Noah steals the cash from Sowerberry's till, heads for London and falls in with Fagin, who sends him to spy on Nancy's movements. Noah sees her meet Brownlow and reports back – with fatal results.

***DAWKINS, JACK (VIII)**, the **ARTFUL DODGER**, whose native guile earns him this soubriquet, is prominent in Fagin's ring

117

of pickpockets. Aged about 11. Bowlegged and short for his age (4ft 6in), sturdy, snub-nosed, "little sharp ugly eyes" and "roystering and swaggering" manner, conducts himself like a grown man, smokes pipes and wears a hat and a coat much too large for him.

He meets Oliver when he is on the run and recruits him for the gang. Police catch Dawkins with a silver snuffbox in his possession; he gives a characteristically swashbuckling performance in court but is nevertheless sent down.

***FAGIN (VIII)**, runs a ring of pickpockets; he is also a fence for jewellery and other stolen goods; "a very old shrivelled Jew", villainous and repulsive face, matted red hair, as dirty as his home, gleefully teaches Oliver what seems a jolly game with handkerchiefs but which is in fact a lesson in picking pockets. Bullies his boys when they do not steal enough and is livid when Oliver escapes. He also recruited girls for prostitution, including Nancy. When the gang collapses he is caught and hanged.

FANG (XI), evil-tempered police magistrate with stern and much-flushed face and intimidating manner, tries to have Oliver jailed.

MAYLIE, ROSE (XXIX), 17, intelligent, "mild and gentle, pure and beautiful", takes loving charge of Oliver after the burglary and restores him to health.

She has been given a home by Mrs Maylie and taken her name, but rejects offer of marriage from Mrs Maylie's son Harry because he is to enter Parliament and her illegitimate birth would harm his career. When Oliver's background is revealed it comes out that she is his aunt – the sister of Oliver's dead mother. Harry returns and when he says he has given up politics for the Church she accepts him.

MONKS (XXXIX), feckless half-brother of Oliver. He knew that his father, equally feckless, died an untimely death before he could marry Oliver's mother. Monks sought to conceal the truth in order to keep Oliver from his inheritance.

***NANCY (IX)**, young woman with a very free manner and "a great deal of colour in her face". Bill Sikes's woman, she loves him despite "a life of suffering and ill-usage". Fagin had put her on the streets 12 years before. She kidnaps the escaped Oliver and restores him to Fagin's den, but he arouses her compassion and she regrets her "life of sin and sorrow".

She meets Brownlow and Rose Maylie secretly to bring Oliver back to them; when she returns Sikes murders her.

***SIKES, BILL (XIII)**, stoutly built burglar of about 35, drab breeches, brown hat, surly temper, scowling eyes. Shares robbery proceeds with Fagin. Always accompanied by faithful white dog Bull's-eye, which he treats badly. Bungles a burglary in Chertsey, flees carrying injured Oliver but drops him to get away. When Noah Claypole tells Sikes of Nancy's meeting with Brownlow he clubs her to death and flees. He tries to kill his dog, which makes a getaway – and leads him back to London, docklands and trouble. Chased by the multitude, and trying to lower himself from a roof to safety in the Thames mud, the rope slips round his neck and he hangs himself. The dog, also on the roof, falls to its death

***TWIST, OLIVER (I)**, eponymous hero. Nameless woman has a child, kisses it and dies. The new baby, named Oliver Twist by parish beadle Bumble, grows up miserably, a pauper in the workhouse. By the age of nine he is "a pale thin child diminutive in stature".

When the starving orphans get together and draw lots Oliver draws the lot to do a bold deed: he goes to the man handing out the gruel and asks, "Please Sir, I want some more." He is put into solitary confinement and flogged. The workhouse apprentices him to undertaker Sowerberry, where he is again starved. When the other apprentice Claypole taunts Olive about his mother Oliver knocks him down. Oliver is thrashed and absconds.

On the way to London he is picked up by petty thief the Artful Dodger and taken to Fagin's den, where he is taught how to pick pockets by Fagin pretending it is all a game. On his first expedition out he sees Dodger stealing the handkerchief of bookshop browser Mr Brownlow, realises what the "game" really is and panics. He is caught and hauled into court before the malignant magistrate Fang.

Brownlow realises Oliver's innocence, takes him home and has him nursed back to health. On his first errand for Mr Brownlow Oliver is kidnapped by Nancy and returned to Fagin's den. He is sent to help Sikes and an accomplice to burgle a house in Chertsey; the raid is badly bungled, a member of the staff shoots Oliver in the arm; Sikes takes Oliver on his back and flees but eventually drops Oliver into the ditch.

Oliver wakes and goes to seek help. He finds himself back at the house of the burglary, where the staff want to turn him in, but young Rose Maylie nurses him back to health. On settlement of his affairs Oliver inherits £3,000, is adopted by Brownlow and lives with him near the parsonage of Rose and her clergyman husband Harry.

OUR MUTUAL FRIEND

★★★**BOFFIN, NICODEMUS or "NODDY" (Bk 1, V)**, a broad round-shouldered little man with bright eager grey eyes, is, with the non-appearance of the heir from the Cape, the keeper of the Harmon fortune, built up by its late founder Harmon senior from dust, scrap and rubbish collection. He had been a foreman in the firm; he and his loving wife Henrietty are "honest and true".

He is a friendly jolly man who regrets that "all print is shut to me" and with his new affluence feels the need for some learning, hence his hiring of street vendor Silas Wegg to teach him to read.

He visits the Temple chambers of the solicitor Mortimer Lightwood, who tells him that now the will of Harmon *père* has been proved, and the son being dead, Mr Boffin has inherited an estate worth over £100,000. Boffin immediately lays down that a reward of £10,000 be offered for the conviction of the murderer of the man found in the Thames.

On leaving Lightwood's, he is accosted by Rokesmith *(who IS the missing heir)*, who asks him to give him a job as secretary as Boffin will now need help to manage his affairs.

Boffin and his wife go to visit the home of the poor Wilfer family and invite the eldest daughter Bella to come and live with them because they want other people, too, to benefit from their new wealth. Mr Boffin asks Mrs Wilfer about her lodger Rokesmith, and adds: "What sort of a fellow is Our Mutual Friend?" She says she is satisfied with him.

Rokesmith becomes Boffin's secretary and when he and the Boffins go to visit the old Harmon mansion where the Boffins intend to live, the older man and his wife reminisce about how they used to comfort lonely little John Harmon – not knowing the identity of the man sitting in front of them.

Rokesmith handles the Boffins' affairs with smooth self-effacing competence, even when Boffin starts turning mean and rude. Miserliness seems to become a sudden obsession, much to the dismay of Mrs Boffin.

Boffin comes one evening to the mounds of dust and scrap in the Harmon estate and, while Wegg and Venus secretly watch in the hope of learning something to their advantage, they see him retrieve a square bottle from one of the mounds and take it away.

Confidence trickster Sophronia Lammle poisons Boffin's mind against Rokesmith, claiming that as the secretary wants to marry Bella Wilfer he is a self-seeker not to be trusted and should be sacked (giving an opportunity for Lammle to fill the vacancy and retrieve his fortunes). She has success in that Boffin calls Rokesmith in, insults hims so grossly that his wife and Bella are led to protest, and sacks him. Bella calls Boffin "a hard-hearted miser" and leaves the house to return to the Wilfer family.

Boffin is rudely summoned to meet Wegg and Venus; they tell him about a previous will, which would leave him penniless. He accepts it meekly.

His one-time employee Rokesmith at last appearing in his real guise as John Harmon, there is joy all round – and the Boffins do not seem to mind that their mansion will now be taken over by the rightful heir. Boffin makes it plain that his rudeness and miserliness were an act to test Bella's character; that she had sided with the secretary proves her worth.

Wegg comes to claim his "inheritance" and is told by the newly revealed Harmon that in the square bottle recovered by Boffin was another will – rendering Wegg's will worthless.

The final settlement: Harmon collects the estate, Boffin the generous legacy left to him in the original will. Wegg is thrown out of the house and lands in a scavenger's cart.

FLEDGEBY, "FASCINATION" (Bk 2, IV), age 23, "awkward, sandy-haired, small-eyed youth" so timid and dull that his friends ironically call him "Fascination" Fledgeby.

He has promised to pay the Lammles a fee if they can arrange his marriage to the heiress Georgiana Podsnap, who is being groomed by Sophronia. However, the courtship is slow: both parties are tongue-tied, despite the Lammles' efforts.

Fledgeby, although socially so backward, is uninhibited when it comes to his passion, wealth. In the City he is a money-lending racketeer but uses as his frontman an elderly Jewish merchant called Mr Riah.

Fledgeby asks about Lizzie Hexam and Mr Riah says that he has moved her to a place of the country because Wrayburn's approach to her has made him fear for her virtue.

Sophronia comes to plead with Fledgeby for time to pay their debts. Fledgeby promises to do what he can, making her cringingly grateful, then goes straight to Riah to tell him to enforce the bill. Having been reduced to penury, her husband Alfred thrashes Fledgeby before leaving London.

Now he has no further use for Riah, Fledgeby dismisses him. The old man, now destitute, is given a home by the dolls' dressmaker Jenny Wren.

HANDFORD, JULIUS (Bk 1, III), *is the pseudonym chosen by John Harmon who has come back from the Cape knowing that, under his father's will, to collect the Harmon family fortune he has to marry Bella Wilfer, whom he does not know. He gives out that John Harmon has been drowned and goes to view what is given out to be "his" body, found in the river by Thames waterman Jesse Hexam. He then changes his identity again: see JOHN ROKESMITH.*

★★★HEADSTONE, BRADLEY (Bk 2, I), aged 26, looks a decent young man dressed in sober black, and is a "highly certificated schoolmaster" who has risen from poverty by hard work and mechanical application to his duties. Hard-headed, snobbish, deeply insecure, he seeks to draw his star pupil Charley Hexam away from Charley's sister Lizzie because of Lizzie's work with her father.

When he meets Lizzie he is drawn to her; she immediately mistrusts him. He goes to Wrayburn's chambers in the Temple with Charley so that the boy can tell Wrayburn not to pay for Lizzie's education but leave it to Headstone. Wrayburn refuses and is so offhand and contemptuous that the schoolmaster is "white with passion".

Headstone twice visits Lizzie in an attempt to woo her, speaks passionately about his feelings and desperately asks for some hope for the future. She refuses firmly. He leaves her with his face deadly white.

He tells Rokesmith of his dislike of Wrayburn and again his face is distorted with violent feeling.

He begins to stalk Wrayburn, who takes long evening walks from the Temple deliberately to provoke the man who he knows is following him. Headstone becomes like an "ill-tamed wild animal" and at the end of another night of stalking he is "ridden hard by evil spirits". In this mood he meets Rogue Riderhood and urges him to help find Lizzie.

In the summer, when Wrayburn takes his skiff up river, Headstone stalks him again in the hope that the lawyer will lead him to Lizzie. He is put up by Riderhood, now a lock-keeper who has also been treated contemptuously by Wrayburn: they nurse a common hatred.

Headstone attacks Wrayburn and leaves him for dead. Back home, he resumes sober garb and school role. By chance he meets a clergyman who says he is to perform a marriage ceremony; he collapses when, though no names are mentioned, he realises the truth; apparently his love Lizzie is marrying Wrayburn.

Riderhood seeks to blackmail the schoolmaster. Headstone comes to meet him by the lock, Riderhood says he will drain him dry. The schoolmaster replies: "I'll hold you living and I'll hold you dead." Headstone grapples with him, they fall into the lock. Their bodies are found by the lock gates.

HEXAM, CHARLEY (Bk 1, III), about 15 when the story begins, lives with father and sister by the riverside. When his father finds a body in the Thames, Charley goes to fetch the lawyer Mortimer Lightwood and his friend and brings them both to his father.

His sister Lizzie tells Charley it is best to secure his future by escaping the family home and going to school. He becomes an adept pupil in a school on the Kent/Surrey border, where Bradley Headstone is head.

Charley goes to see his sister, finds her as lodger of the crippled dolls' dressmaker Jenny Wren, and feels this is not smart enough. He saddens her by upbraiding her for living there. Later, he angrily goes to Wrayburn's chambers to urge her vainly to get her education from Headstone and not Wrayburn.

Charley finds a new job at another school and after the news of the attack on Wrayburn comes to Headstone, looks reproachful and says he feels "tainted" by his acquaintance with the headmaster because he was responsible for bringing him into contact with Wrayburn.

HEXAM, JESSE (Bk 1, I), strongly built with grizzled hair and "a wildness of beard and whisker", a waterman who makes his living from bodies he fishes up out of the Thames. The opening scene in the novel finds him in his skiff between Southwark Bridge and London Bridge. He picks up a body in the water and rifles the pockets. His fellow waterman Roger Riderhood, with whom he has fallen out, tells the lawyer Lightwood that Hexam murdered Harmon; with police help they go looking for Hexham on the river and find him drowned.

***HEXAM, LIZZIE (Bk 1, I), aged 19 or 20, Hexham's daughter, helps him in his river work scavenging for bodies, a job she hates. She is close to her young brother and has arranged for him to learn to read and write.

After her father drowns, she moves in with the dolls' dressmaker Jenny Wren, in a house near St John's Smith Square, and earns a living as a needlewoman. She is visited by Charley and Headstone and takes a prompt dislike to Headstone; she is miserable when Charley, now ambitious about his career, tries to draw her away from living with a cripple like Jenny Wren.

Lizzie and Jenny are called on by Wrayburn, who refers to himself as "a bad idle dog" and in an act of generosity arranges to get them a tutor.

Lizzie has two admirers, neither of whom has declared himself: Eugene Wrayburn and Bradley Headstone.

Headstone twice tries to talk her round, without success, leaving her with his face deadly white. Lizzie dismisses him to Jenny as "a very strange man".

Lizzie leaves her home with Jenny Wren at Mr Riah's behest; Riah says that he fears for her virtue if she stays within reach of Wrayburn and has moved her into the country. However, when she meets Bella she tells her that she had Riah take her away because she was frightened of Headstone. She confesses that she loves a man who is far above her socially but that her love runs deep – she means Wrayburn but does not name him.

Wrayburn tracks her to her place in the country and she pleads with him not to pursue her as their social backgrounds are too far apart.

Reluctantly he leaves her; he is attacked by Headstone; she finds him floating unconscious in the water, gets a boat and with her old river skill rescues him, obtains medical help and saves his life.

Jenny Wren learns that Wrayburn wishes to marry Lizzie before he dies; a clergyman is fetched to perform the ceremony at his bedside and he recovers.

They are married; Lizzie shares in the work of Wrayburn's convalescence.

LAMMLE, ALFRED (Bk 1, X), confidence trickster who marries the "mature young lady" Sophronia with ostentatious ceremony at the Veneering mansion. They go on honeymoon and immediately discover they have both been deceived by the snobbish Veneering as to wealth: in fact she has little money and he none at all.

Alfred tells her mutual reproaches will not get them anywhere; they should develop a "mutual understanding" to work together to pursue money. Their first intended victim: the simple-minded heiress Georgiana Podsnap.

That plot fails (due to Sophronia's action, of which her husband knows nothing) and they ponder what next they can do to avoid bankruptcy. They agree that Sophronia will tell Mr Boffin confidentially that Secretary Rokesmith has made his feelings to Miss Wilfer plain and is therefore not to be trusted; dismiss him and Lammle can become Boffin's secretary. The ploy does not work; though Rokesmith loses his job Boffin does not put the job of secretary on offer and simply pays the Lammles £100 to get rid of them.

As his last act in London, Lammle soundly thrashes Fledgeby and emigrates with his wife to Calais.

LAMMLE, SOPHRONIA (Bk 1, XX), the "mature young lady" (i.e. not as young as she gives out to be) and schemer who marries Alfred Lammle with a view to making a good match and finds he has even less money than she has (she has an annuity of £150 a year). He tells her they should work together to pursue money: she starts by flattering the naïve heiress Georgiana Podsnap to get her to marry fortune-hunter Fledgeby.

She has a change of heart and at a Lammle dinner party quietly urges Fledgeby's cousin Twemlow to speak to Georgiana's father and save her from the marriage, which is just "a money speculation".

Her next intended victim is Bella Wilfer, whom she tells that her beauty must be utilised to make a good match. Bella half-mistrusts Sophronia, and is half taken in because when in a greedy mood she still loves money herself.

Sophronia tells Boffin secretly that Rokesmith is not to be trusted; her poison works and Rokesmith is sacked – but despite pressure and flattery from both Lammles the job of secretary is not offered to her husband. They are given £100 and sent away.

***LIGHTWOOD, MORTIMER (Bk 1, II), "indolent" young solicitor with chambers in the Temple, is a guest at Veneering's dinner and relates some hot gossip going round town: a youth called Harmon goes abroad in disgrace, makes money in the Cape and comes back a grown man to find that his wealthy father has died and left a will stipulating the son must marry a certain young woman in England to inherit the fortune; if he does not, the estate passes to an employee (Boffin).

Lightwood has just finished the story when he is handed a note saying that the very man he has been talking about has been found drowned. The message comes from the young son of the Thames waterman Jesse Hexam who recovered the body.

Lightwood and his barrister friend Wrayburn are taken by the boy to Rotherhithe, speak to Jesse and go to view the body. While they are still there an agitated young man breaks in and asks after the body. He refuses to give his reason for coming but gives his name as Julius Handford.

An inquest is held, which Lightwood and Wrayburn attend. The jury finds that a steamer passenger called Harmon was found dead in the river after being badly injured. A reward £100 is posted for solution of the mystery of the "The Harmon Murder".

Lightwood is called in by Veneering to act as best man at Lammle's wedding.

Lightwood, at home in his quarters with Wrayburn, is visited by Thames waterman Riderhood, who claims the reward for the Harmon murder and says that not only did Hexam murder John Harmon but admitted as much to himself. The two men and Riderhood go first to the police and then set out for the river to search; they find Hexam drowned.

Lightwood is in Wrayburn's chambers rooms in the Temple when they are visited by Charley Hexam and the schoolmaster Headstone. Charlie fails to persuade Wrayburn to stop paying for Lizzie's education. After they have left Mortimer quizzes his friend about his feelings for Lizzie and Wrayburn denies he wants to seduce or to marry her.

When Wrayburn is at death's door after being attacked by Headstone, Lightwood comes to fetch Jenny Wren to his bedside and says of the relationship with Wrayburn: "We have long been much more than brothers." He fetches a clergyman to marry Lizzie and Wrayburn.

Back in town, Lightwood chances to meet in the street Bella and her husband, the man he last saw as the agitated Julius Handford at the inquest on the body in the Thames. Explanations are urgently called for and given: Rokesmith admits at last that he is the missing heir John Harmon.

PODSNAP, GEORGIANA (Bk 1, XI), Mr Podsnap's over-protected teenage daughter, an innocent heiress over whom the confidence trickster Sophronia Lammle soon establishes a hold. There is a commission from Fledgeby if she can persuade Georgiana to marry him; there is little prospect of this, given the girl's reaction even to his presence.

Sophronia relents, and at a dinner party she draws Twemlow, a cousin of Fledgeby's, aside and tells him that he should warn his friend Podsnap against letting his daughter marry Fledgeby as "she is on the brink of being sold into wretchedness for life".

While the Lammles are in the Boffin home vainly urging Mr Boffin to take Alfred on as secretary, Georgiana bursts in, commiserates tearfully with Sophronia and offers them generous gifts and says she intends to turn over her entire estate to the Lammles. Boffin quietly takes possession of the gifts to return them to Georgiana's father, and hands the Lammles £100 to get rid of them.

PODSNAP, JOHN (Bk 1, II), a "large man with a fatal freshness on him", is a guest at Veneering's dinner party. "Eminently respectable", he considers other nations a mistake, their manners and customs unacceptable as "not English".

Tipped off that Fledgeby is not a suitable husband for his daughter, he writes to the Lammles that they are no longer socially acceptable.

RIDERHOOD, ROGER (Bk 1, XII), ill-looking Thames waterman who had earlier in the story fallen out with Jesse Hexam, visits the solicitor Lightwood some time after the finding of the body in the Thames. He says that he wants to claim Mr Boffin's £10,000 reward for the Harmon murder as he knows the murderer was Jesse Hexham – and that Hexham himself admitted it. He takes Lightwood and his friend Wrayburn to the police sergeant handling the case; from there on they go along the river front, and find Hexam drowned.

Riderhood becomes lock-keeper upriver at Plaistow Weir further up the Thames. He meets the schoolmaster Headstone, who hopes that this man with his long links with the Hexams can help him find Lizzie; Riderhood agrees to try.

When Wrayburn sculls upriver in his skiff he is stalked by Headstone, who hopes that the barrister will lead him to Lizzie. Headstone is put up for the night in Riderhood's cabin – two men with a common hatred of Wrayburn.

Weeks after the attack, Riderhood, who knows what has happened, seeks to blackmail Headstone. The schoolmaster comes to see him by the lock; Headstone grapples with him; their bodies are found by the lock gates.

★★★ROKESMITH, JOHN (Bk 1, IV), the hero of the novel. He begins life as little Johnny Harmon, son of the London dust-and-rubbish tycoon and "tremendous old rascal" John Harmon. The child is often fondly dandled on the knee of Mrs Boffin, whose husband is the foreman of Harmon senior.

Father and son fall out, the son goes to the Cape, becomes a wine-grower and spends 14 years there. His father dies and he hears that the will stipulates the son can inherit everything provided he marries a certain girl who was only a child when the will was drawn up years ago, later identified as Bella Wilfer. If he does not marry her, the entire estate goes to the one-time foreman, already identified as Nicodemus Boffin.

"I came back, shrinking from my father's memory, mistrustful of being forced on a mercenary wife." His only happy memories were of two "dear, noble, honest friends": the Boffins.

On board the vessel bringing him back to England he meets a man "alike in bulk and stature" with whom he becomes friendly and to whom he confides his good fortune. After some time ashore they meet again by the riverside; soon afterwards Harmon remembers he was drugged, fell in the Thames and somehow managed to save himself.

Days later, calling himself Julius Handford, he goes to a police station and there sees the body of a man who had also come to grief, his lookalike, robbed for the money for which he would have murdered Harmon. He identifies the body as "Harmon".

He sees a placard in Whitehall about John Harmon having been mutilated and murdered in dockland. The body is buried, the reward is out for the perpetrator of the "Harmon Murder".

He abandons the role of Handford and considers if he should have Harmon come back to life. He decides against: it would now be too upsetting for everyone – and so he calls himself John Rokesmith.

He is not yet 30 years old, a dark man with an "expressive handsome face". He looks troubled and diffident as he enters the Wilfer household as their new first-floor lodger, wanting to see what his intended bride is like.

When Boffin has been told that he has the family fortune, Rokesmith approaches him in the street and offers to act as his secretary.

The Boffins go to ask the Wilfers if their eldest daughter would like to go and live with them and then ask about the Wilfers' lodger; Mr Boffin adds: "What sort of fellow is Our Mutual Friend?" Mrs Wilfer says he is "punctual, quiet and eligible".

The Boffins, childless for years, announce that they also want to adopt a little boy and give him a good chance in life, referring to the prospective addition as "my little John Harmon", at which Rokesmith turns pale.

Rokesmith is accepted as secretary and he and the Boffins go to the grand Harmon mansion where they are now to live. Boffin enthuses to Rokesmith about the old days when he and his wife often comforted the shy little boy Harmon.

The secretary soon falls in love with the girl his father's will enjoined him to marry, Bella. She tells him that she is embarrassed because he is Boffin's employee, and urges him to "discontinue your habit of making your misplaced attentions as plain to Mrs Boffin as to me."

Boffin begins to turn miserly and overbearing; he tells Rokesmith he must immediately move into his home to be always at hand. Rokesmith remains the perfect secretary, courteous and dispassionate and hiding his humiliation at Boffin's constant bullying. His self-control impresses Bella. Her atttitude to him becomes warm and friendly. When he reveals his feelings and proposes marriage she rejects him.

Mrs Lammle poisons Boffin's mind against Rokesmith in the hope that her husband may get Rokesmith's job as secretary. A ready victim, Boffin promptly sacks Rokesmith, who denies mercenary motives in wooing Bella, stresses he still loves her and departs, leaving Bella to reproach Boffin and leave the house as well and go to her father. Rokesmith follows her, declares himself again and they become engaged.

They are married and he gives out that he is working in a City trading house at £150 a year. The couple move into a modest cottage in Blackheath. He tells her they might be richer; she says she wishes for nothing more and adds that she expects a child. A daughter is born, also named Bella.

Rokesmith goes into London with his wife and by chance comes face to face with Mortimer Lightwood, who had last met the strange man Julius Handford at the inquest on the murder victim.

Explanations are urgently called for and obtained; John Rokesmith *is* the missing heir John Harmon.

They drive straight to the home of the Boffins, who greet them with beaming smiles. Mrs Boffin says to Bella, "Welcome to your house and home, my deary!"

Silas Wegg comes to claim his "inheritance" and Rokesmith, now in his own character as John Harmon, tells him that the will in the square bottle retrieved by Boffin was yet another will, leaving Wegg's find worthless.

Final settlement: Rokesmith/Harmon collects the estate; Boffin gets the generous legacy originally allocated to him; Wegg is thrown out of the houses and into a scavenger's cart.

TWEMLOW, MELVIN (Bk 1, II), timid, "grey and polite" social butterfly, a regular guest at Veneering social events. At the Lammle wedding he gives the bride away. He becomes one of the election team when Veneering seeks a seat in Parliament. At a Lammle dinner party he is urged by Sophronia to speak to Podsnap *père* to save the "the foolish affectionate" Georgiana from marrying Twemlow's cousin Fledgeby.

VENEERING, HAMILTON (Bk 1, II), aged, 40, "wavy-haired, dark, tending to corpulence", is a social climber in the West End of London with everything in his life brand-new: house, furniture, clothes, plate, servants. Everyone he meets is instantly the oldest and dearest friend. He hosts a dinner with selected society guests; among them are the lawyers Mortimer Lightwood and Eugene Wrayburn. It is at this dinner that Mortimer tells the assembled company of the Harmon estate and the fate of its heir.

Veneering hosts the wedding breakfast for the Lammles, having out of pride misrepresented to both bride and groom that the other is rich.

He seeks a career in Parliament and with extensive help from "oldest and dearest friends" he becomes the MP for Pocket Breaches.

When the Lammles go bankrupt, a "total smash", they are no longer the oldest and dearest friends, and Veneering's other friends go to the sale of the Lammles' possessions.

Veneering ges bankrupt, takes the Chiltern Hundreds and retires to Calais with his wife.

WEGG, SILAS (Bk 1, V), a vendor offering "half-penny ballads" and fruits and nuts in a "sterile little stall" on a street corner. Mr Boffin comes to him and believing him to be a learned man because of the ballads offers him a job as part-time tutor to teach the illiterate Mr Boffin how to read at a fee of five shillings a week.

Wegg becomes in fact "a handsomely-remunerated humbug"; secretly he wants to profiteer from his employer and soon establishes a hold over him. Wegg moves into Boffin's old house where he spends much time prodding and probing in the house and in the dust mounds as if in the expectation of finding something. He finds a confederate in a taxidermist friend Venus and they agree to split between them any advantage they may find.

In a hidden money-box Wegg finds a late will in which Harmon stipulates that after a legacy to Boffin all the rest of the estate should revert to the Crown.

Wegg and Venus agree that they should bide their time and when the moment is ripe blackmail Boffin into paying them to suppress this will. Soon each man plots to cheat his partner.

When Rokesmith has assumed his real identity as Harmon, Wegg goes to claim under the will he found and is told (by Harmon) that it is worthless as another will retrieved by Boffin is the real one.

The final settlement of the estate goes to Harmon and Boffin; Wegg is thrown out of the house and into a scavenger's cart.

★★★WILFER, BELLA (Bk 1, IV), eldest daughter of Runty Wilfer, aged about 19, brown hair, brown eyes, with an "exceedingly pretty figure and face" but with "a petulant expression". She wears black even though, as she protested, she was never married: she wears mourning for the death of her fiancé, John Harmon, reported drowned in the Thames, an "intended husband left to her like a dozen of spoons".

The family take in a new lodger, John Rokesmith, and when he cannot give any references she tells her father that he might well be a murderer, little knowing that the man she speaks of is the same "intended husband".

Mr and Mrs Boffin feel she would have a better future sharing with them in their new wealth and invite her to come and live with them. Boffin asks Mrs Wilfer whether she has a lodger and adds "What sort of fellow is Our Mutual Friend?" Mrs Wilfer tells him that Rokesmith is "punctual, quiet and eligible".

With the Boffins moving into their new home, Bella moves out of her parents' house and joins them as their live-in guest. It is not long before the new secretary, Mr Rokesmith, shows his feelings towards her; she tells him to cease his "misplaced attentions".

Mrs Lammle cultivates her and tells her she can with her beauty make a good marriage, which feeds into Bella's tendency to be mercenary – for which she often reproaches herself.

She has a long talk with Lizzie Hexam and confesses she loves a man. Lizzie's kindly attitude makes Bella warm to her and feel that she herself is often just capricious; she has a change in attitude and when she next meets Rokesmith again she is as engaging and relaxed as she used to be. In this better atmosphere he again tells her that he loves her; she turns him down.

Boffin, a victim to Sophronia Lammle's plotting, dismisses Rokesmith and in such intemperate terms that Bella is shocked. As Rokesmith leaves she tenders a tearful apology that "you laid yourself open to be slighted by a worldly shallow girl".

She leaves the Boffin house and goes to her father's office, where Rokesmith, with concealment no longer necessary, follows her and declares himself again; she, aware she was wrong in her mercenary attitudes and now "so thankful and so happy", accepts him.

They are married and he gives out that he works in the City. He mentions that they could be richer than they are now but she says that, now she is no longer greedy in temperament, she wishes for nothing. And so he does not reveal himself. They have a daughter, also called Bella.

When the couple by chance meet Mortimer Lightwood in a London street and explanations are called for, Bella learns the true identity of her husband. They go to live in the big house and entertain to dinner Mrs Eugene Wrayburn and her husband, who slowly recovers.

WILFER, REGINALD ("RUNTY") (Bk 1, IV), a poor clerk with the "chubby smooth innocent appearance" of a cherub living with his domineering "majestic" wife and their large family in Holloway. He is an employee in the Veneering drug business and has a kind and patient manner.

He is unhappily married and has therefore a special bond with his eldest daughter, Bella, who takes him on a happy excursion to Greenwich; he is surprised when she comes back to him after denouncing Boffin for his treatment of Rokesmith.

He readily accepts his daughter's engagement to Rokesmith, good-naturedly assessing that her avarice mode has deserted her. He leaves his bossy wife at home while he happily attends his daughter's wedding.

★★★WRAYBURN, EUGENE (Bk 1, II), barrister guest at the Veneering dinner party and old school friend of Lightwood's. The two young men go to Jesse Hexam to hear how the "Harmon" body was found and attend the inquest the next day.

He takes part in the hunt that ends in finding Jesse Hexam's body.

After Jesse's death he visits Lizzie and, anxious to do something positive in his life, offers to provide her with a teacher.

Lightwood is with him in his rooms in the Temple when they are visited by Charley Hexam and the headmaster Headstone. The boy tells Wrayburn to stop paying for his sister Lizzie's schooling as it could be better undertaken by Headstone.

Wrayburn refuses and treats Headstone so contemptuously that Headstone is "white with passion" and warns him that if Wrayburn does not lay off Lizzie "you will find me as bitterly in earnest against you as I could be". After they leave without success Mortimer teases his friend about his feelings for Lizzie and Wrayburn denies he wants to seduce or to marry her.

Headstone begins to stalk Wrayburn, who takes long, rambling nightly walks in order to distress the man whom he knows is following him. Lightwood assesses Headstone's state of mind and is much more worried; Wrayburn laughs it off.

In high summer, Wrayburn takes a skiff to row up river and has to pass through a lock manned by Rogue Riderhood, leaving the lock-keeper cursing when Wrayburn loftily expresses the wish that he may be soon "transported or hanged".

Wrayburn does not notice that he is still being stalked by Headstone, who is convinced that the barrister will lead him to Lizzie's hideaway; Headstone is put up by Riderhood in his lock-side cabin – two men with a common hatred of Wrayburn.

Wrayburn meets Lizzie on a towpath; she tells him that he is too far removed from her socially and that he should withdraw from her; he says goodbye and reflects he would be less of an aimless drifter if he married her.

In a lonely spot Wrayburn is badly beaten by Headstone and left for dead in the river. Lizzie happens to come past, sees his body and pale face in the stream, gets him to medical help and saves his life.

He is helpless in his sickroom for a long time, attended constantly by Lizzie, Lightwood and Jenny Wren. He tells Lightwood that Headstone must never be exposed as his attacker because Lizzie's name would come out and her reputation would suffer. Jenny Wren discovers that Wrayburn's secret wish is to marry Lizzie before he dies. Lightwood undertakes to make the arrangements; Wrayburn in confiding in his friend tells him, "Touch my face with yours. I love you, Mortimer."

Lightwood brings in a clergyman and the couple are married. Wrayburn speaks to his new wife Lizzie of his "trifling idle youth"; the new Mrs Wrayburn speaks of a new "mine of purpose and energy" he will have when he recovers.

He does recover – slowly – and during his convalescence comes to dinner with Mr and Mrs John Harmon.

WREN, JENNY (Bk 2, I), small crippled woman in her twenties with beautiful long golden hair, a dolls' dressmaker by trade with her home near St John's Smith Square. Greatly dedicated to her work, she is always seated in a low armchair because her "back is so bad and my legs are queer". Jenny is a strong-minded woman who refers to herself as "the person of the house". Lizzie Hexam has moved in as her lodger after Jesse Hexam's death.

Jenny offers the elderly Riah a home when he is made destitute by Fledgeby sacking him.

After Wrayburn is attacked by Headstone, Lightwood comes to fetch Jenny to come and see his friend as he may be dying. Jenny stays by Wrayburn's bedside, nurses and comforts him and discovers his murmured wish: to marry Lizzie.

Harmon having come into his inheritance, he sees to it that Jenny's future is made secure. She finds an admirer in a gentle and good-natured youth called Sloppy she first met through the Boffins.

PICKWICK PAPERS

BARDELL, MRS MARTHA (XII), Mr Pickwick's comely landlady, a widow "with bustling manners and agreeable appearance" in his apartments in Goswell Street, misinterprets his innocent question to her about "the expense of keeping two people rather than one" as a proposal, bursts into tears, falls into his arms and faints. He was in fact seeking advice about hiring a manservant, but Mrs Bardell sues for breach of promise of marriage as she had "long worshipped him at a distance". In the trial of Bardell and Pickwick, the jury finds for the plaintiff and sets the damages at £750.

As Mr Pickwick refuses to pay, after three months Mrs Bardell's solicitors Messrs Dodson and Fogg have their own client seized for payment of their costs. Mrs Bardell is taken to the Fleet prison. On arrival, she sees Mr Pickwick and faints. Mr Pickwick pays the costs involved to secure everyone's release.

Mrs Bardell continues to take in single men as lodgers but is never again involved in a breach of promise case.

★★★JINGLE, ALFRED (II), tall and slim young man in battered green coat; unemployed actor; he has a voluble manner and tells tall stories in distinctively telegraphic sentences.

He attaches himself to the Pickwickians and as an opportunistic itinerant it is thanks to his being in their company that he is given hospitality at Wardle's Manor Farm. He borrows 10 pounds off Tupman – and uses this to fund his flight with the middle-aged spinster Rachael Wardle. In London he has just got a marriage licence when Mr Pickwick and Mr Wardle catch up with him, buy him off with £120 and take Miss Wardle home.

They then pursue Jingle first to Bury and then to Ipswich, where he has been presenting himself as heroic "Captain Fitz-Marshall" and again seeking moneyed women to marry. In the mansion of the Ipswich magistrate he and his helper Job Trotter are confronted with the Pickwickians, unmasked and thrown down the front steps.

When Mr Pickwick is committed to Fleet prison for debt, he meets Jingle and Trotter, now very shabby and at an even lower ebb than before. Jingle makes a determined attempt at flippancy about his situation but breaks down and weeps. His health has suffered and he walks with a stick; Mr Pickwick gets him a private room and releases his clothes from the pawnbroker's.

When he is released himself he secures the freedom of Jingle and Trotter as well. Mr Pickwick secures for both men a passage to the West Indies and a new life.

JOE (IV), the "fat boy", good-natured teenage servant of Mr Wardle at Manor Farm, always in attendance, always falling asleep. He comes to London with Mr Wardle, becomes an agent in the romance between Mr Snodgrass and Emily Wardle and stays awake long enough to tell Emily's pretty servant how much he likes her; when she leaves he eats a large steak – and goes back to sleep.

★★★PICKWICK, SAMUEL (I), genial bespectacled chairman of the club which bears his name, presides at a meeting of the United Pickwickians in the opening chapter. He is a man of ample means.

It is decided to set up for research purposes a travel group which will report from time to time "authenticated accounts of the journeys and observations" on where it goes, the group to be called the Corresponding Society of the Pickwick Club and to be made up of himself, Tracy Tupman, Augustus Snodgrass and Nathaniel Winkle.

Mr Pickwick tells the meeting that they had selected him for "a service of great honour and some danger", as "travelling was in a troubled state". He and his three companions set out on 13 May 1827. They are soon joined by the green-coated man Mr Jingle.

The Pickwickians go to a ball in Rochester and attend a military review where they meet the genial Mr Wardle, owner of Manor Farm at Dingley Dell, who invites them to come and stay. They attend the cricket match between Dingley Dell and All-Muggleton.

He and Mr Wardle pursue Jingle when the fortune-hunter has fled with Wardle's sister Rachael. They catch up with the couple and buy Jingle off.

In his apartments in Goswell Street Mr Pickwick asks his buxom landlady Mrs Bardell her opinion as to the "expense of keeping two people rather than one". It transpires he is considering hiring a manservant, but Mrs Bardell (long in love with Mr Pickwick) misinterprets this as a proposal of marriage, breaks down in tears, embraces Mr Pickwick and faints. In this situation he is discovered by Messrs Snodgrass, Tupman and Winkle.

Sam Weller is fetched from his South London inn and is engaged as a manservant for £12 and two suits a year. He promptly accompanies his new employer and the other Pickwickians to observe the by-election in Eatanswill.

They are invited to a party by the local socialite and cultural lion Mrs Leo Hunter, where Mr Pickwick is made a great fuss of until he hears another guest being announced whose voice is all too familiar: Alfred Jingle. Jingle recognises Mr Pickwick and leaves hurriedly.

Mr Pickwick goes indignantly in pursuit to prevent anyone else falling victim to confidence trickery. On arrival in Bury he and Sam Weller are deceived into believing that Jingle is planning another elopement; as Mr Pickwick goes out to confront him it turns out that Jingle has eluded them.

A letter arrives from London solicitors Messrs Dodson & Fogg, who inform Mr Pickwick they are acting for Mrs Bardell in an action for breach of promise of marriage claiming damages of £1,500. He visits their offices in Cornhill and finds they are sharp practitioners in their profession: he berates them soundly and is rescued from making possibly actionable statements by being pulled away by Sam Weller. He makes contact with the clerk of his own solicitor, Mr Perker.

He meets Sam's father, who says Jingle is now in Ipswich. Mr Pickwick and Sam travel on Weller senior's coach to Ipswich. The men they sought are found: in the mansion of Mr Nupkins, local magistrate, Jingle and his helper are confronted by Mr Pickwick, exposed and kicked down the front steps.

The Pickwickians go to Manor Farm for Christmas and at the Christmas Eve party Mr Pickwick is particularly gallant to Mr Wardle's old mother. The Pickwickians go skating with mixed results; Mr Pickwick falls through the ice, is bundled off to bed with hot punch and recovers remarkably.

The case Bardell and Pickwick comes to trial: Winkle, Snodgrass and Tupman all give evidence that they saw Mrs Bardell faint in the arms of Mr Pickwick and the jury finds in her favour. Damages are set at £750 plus costs, which Mr Pickwick says he will not pay.

Mr Pickwick declares he has never been to Bath and so for their next expedition the Pickwickians travel there. Once there, their leader gallantly acts as intermediary to further the romance between Mr Winkle and the pretty Arabella Allen, who they had met at Manor Farm (Mr Pickwick looks over a high wall piggy-backed by Sam to assure the lady in the garden that all is above board).

Back in London a sheriff calls on him for non-payment of the Bardell judgment. He is committed to the Fleet prison and after seeing much misery hires a private room for a pound a week. He meets Jingle, very much down at heel and helps him and his accomplice Trotter.

He tells Sam that as it is odd for a gentleman to have a valet in prison it is better to stay away until he gets out but he will pay his wages and take him back when he comes out. Sam arranges with his father to be arraigned for debt himself and so to be admitted to Fleet prison and remain with his employer.

Mr Pickwick tours the prison, sees the misery all round and resolves to remain in his own room. For "three long months" Sam Weller and solicitor Mr Perker urge him to pay his money and secure his release, but Mr Pickwick refuses and his health begins to suffer.

He sees Mrs Bardell arrive, now in the same position as he is. On Perker's advice, he settles the matter – and they all leave prison.

Mr Pickwick goes to Birmingham to plead with Mr Winkle's father to give support to his son after marrying Arabella. Angry at first, eventually he relents and comes to London to support the marriage, much to Mr Pickwick's delight.

Mr Pickwick then tells Sam that, as the Pickwick Club has been dissolved, "my rambles are over" and he now wants only "repose and quiet". He will therefore no longer need Sam but plans to set him up in business so he can marry pretty maidservant Mary. Sam replies that he will stick by Mr Pickwick "and nothin' shall ever perwent it".

Mr Pickwick buys a house in Dulwich, from which Mr Snodgrass and Emily Wardle are married. Sam, always in attendance, marries the Mary he first met on an earlier Pickwickian journey.

Mr Pickwick settles in well, is godfather to numerous little Snodgrasses, Winkles and Trundles – and retains "all his juvenility of spirit".

***SNODGRASS, AUGUSTUS (I)**, one of the four men appointed by the United Pickwickians in the opening chapter to be part of the Corresponding Society of the Pickwick Club, which will report to the club on its travels. Mr Snodgrass has poetic feelings (for much of the story he shares experiences with Mr Pickwick). He secretly courts and wins the hand of Emily Wardle; they are married from the new house Mr Pickwick has moved to in Dulwich.

***TUPMAN, TRACY (I)**, one of the four men appointed by

the United Pickwickians in the opening chapter to be part of the Corresponding Society of the Pickwick Club, which will report to the club on its travels. Mr Tupman is "too susceptible" to "the most interesting and pardonable of human weakneses – love (for much of the story he shares experiences with Mr Pickwick).

Mr Tupman reveals his suspceptibiltiies to the middle-aged Miss Wardle and she reciprocates but he is supplanted by Mr Jingle, who borrows £10 from him and takes the lady away himself. Mr Tupman writes to Mr Pickwick that his loss of this "lovely and fascinating creature" is too much and that he is going; the other Pickwickians feel they must follow him, take their leave of Mr Wardle and head for a Kent village inn, where they are reunited with their friend having overcome suicidal tendencies.

Mr Tupman remains single and never proposes marriage again.

WARDLE, MR (IV), jovial elderly countryman, owner of Manor Farm in Dingley Dell, lives in a spacious farmhouse with a very deaf mother, a sister Rachael ("the spinster aunt") and two daughters, Emily and Arabella. Bella is to marry her suitor Mr Trundle.

Mr Wardle meets the Pickwickians in Rochester and invites them to Manor Farm for country pursuits: a rook shoot and a cricket match.

When he hears that Jingle has fled with his sister Rachael he and Mr Pickwick pursue them but the moonlit chase ends when their coach loses a wheel. The chase is resumed, they locate the couple and buy Jingle off with £120: Miss Rachael is escorted home.

Back at Manor Farm, Mr Wardle sees his daughter Bella married to Mr Trundle and on Christmas Eve hosts a great party attended by the Pickwick party, all the Wardle family and staff, including the below-stairs people and the fat boy Joe.

***WELLER, SAM (X), first discovered cleaning boots at the White Hart inn in south London, where the fleeing Jingle and Rachael Wardle have put up. Mr Wardle bribes him to reveal the whereabouts of the runaways.

Mr Pickwick engages Sam as his manservant at £12 plus two suits a year and Sam goes with the party to see the Eatanswill by-election, then on to Bury in pursuit of Jingle. The plan to entrap Jingle there miscarries. From then on Sam is Mr Pickwick's constant attendant and it becomes clear that his knowledge of London is "extensive and peculiar".

At Bath Sam meets again the pretty housemaid Mary he had met on an earlier Pickwickian expedition.

When Mr Pickwick is confined in Fleet prison for debt, he gently tells Sam that in this strange situation it is better he does not attend him, although his wages will continue to be paid. Sam promptly arranges to borrow money from his father and to have himself arrested for unpaid debt – and thrown into Fleet prison so he can be with his master.

His stepmother dies and leaves him a comfortable legacy with which he will marry Arabella Allen's pretty maid Mary. Mr Pickwick tells him that the Pickwick Club is no more and he will therefore not need Sam's services; Sam stoutly protest that he will never leave Mr Pickwick.

Indeed he doesn't – he moves with him to the new Pickwick headquarters in Dulwich, marries Mary and some years later there are "two sturdy little boys".

WELLER, TONY (XX), Samuel Weller's father, stout elderly red-faced coachman, meets his son and Mr Pickwick in a tavern, hears of their recent contretemps with Jingle, compares notes about their appearance and tells them that their quarry is in Ipswich; Mr Pickwick travels there in the coach of Weller senior.

Mr Weller has taken as second wife a woman who has turned to religion and is in thrall to a bibulous preacher, the "red-nosed Mr. Stiggins". He warns his son to "be wery careful o' widders all your life, Sammy."

His wife dies after catcing cold listening to a sermon. Mr

Stiggins come to call to see if he has been left anything; Mr Weller seizes him and thrusts him head-first into a horse-trough.

Weller receives money from the estate of his late wife and Mr Pickwick invests it for him with such success that when he retires as coachman he goes to live in "an excellent public-house near Shooter's Hill".

★★★**WINKLE, NATHANIEL (I)**, one of the four men appointed by the United Pickwickians in the opening chapter to be part of the Corresponding Society of the Pickwick Club, which will report to the club on its travels. Mr Winkle, dressed in a green shooting coat at the meeting, is interested in sport (for much of the story he shares experiences with Mr Pickwick).

Mr Winkle is called to fight a duel and as he not as bold a sportsman as he likes to give out is much relieved when it turns out to be a case of mistaken identity. His reputation as a horseman suffers when he fails to ride a horse and as a marksman when he goes out in a shooting party, aims at rooks and injures Mr Tupman instead: furiously, Mr Pickwick says "Wretch!"

Asked soon afterwards if he plays cricket, he declines – "modestly". At a partridge shoot he again reveals incompetence with firearms. At the Christmas festivities at Manor Farm he fails again, this time on skates, causing Mr Pickwick to call him a humbug and an impostor.

The Pickwickians go to Bath accompanied by a new acquaintance called Dowler. In Bath, Mrs Dowler goes to a party, comes home late and only Mr Winkle hears the knocking on the door. He goes to the rescue, the wind slams the door behind him and Mr Winkle, to avoid the public, slips into the sedan chair occupied by Mrs Dowler. The whole house is aroused, Mr Dowler misinterprets his wife's situation and threatens violence.

The frightened Mr Winkle flees to Bath in the hope of avoiding the husband's wrath and there meets the husband, who had also fled – just as anxious to avoid violence.

Mr Winkle meets again Arabella Allen, the pretty girl with furlined boots he met at Wardle's. He marries her and takes her to visit Mr Pickwick in prison. Mr Pickwick, after his release, feels responsible for the diffident young man as one of his followers, and goes to Birmingham to see Mr Winkle's father and gain approval of, and financial support for, his son's decision but finds opposition.

Mr Pickwick implies that he is willing to support the young couple himself. Mr Winkle senior travels down from Birmingham, says that he was too hasty and gives his son and Arabella Winkle (née Allen) his blessing. The groom settles down to a new career as a businessman.

★★★★★★★★

NOTE: *Arabella Allen marries Mr Winkle*
      Arabella Wardle marries Mr Trundle
      Emily Wardle marries Mr Snodgrass

★★★★★★★★

A TALE OF TWO CITIES

BARSAD, JOHN (Bk 2, II), prosecution witness at Old Bailey trial in 1780 of Charles Darnay for treason. His evidence is disbelieved after he is accused of being a government spy. Darnay is cleared.

Years later, he is in Paris as a spy for the French authorities. He comes to the Defarge wineshop and tries to draw husband and wife into making subversice comments but they are too wily for him.

Come the Revolution, he is still in Paris, now as a turnkey in a prison. He meets Carton, who pressures him into smuggling him into Darnay's cell just before Darnay is due to be guillotined.

★★★CARTON, SYDNEY (Bk 2 II), barrister with torn gown, untidy wig and disreputable look, is sitting in the Old Bailey at Darnay's trial for treason; as junior defence counsel he passes a note for Lucie Manette from the prisoner and as the two men face each other the resemblance between them is striking. Following the acquittal Carton takes Darnay to dinner at a nearby Fleet Street tavern, feeds Darnay well while he keeps drinking port and refers to himself as a "disappointed drudge". Darnay leaves, and Carton reflects that his guest had made him realise what a better life he (Carton) might have made for himself.

Carton visits the Manettes in their Soho home but is "moody and morose". On a summer evening he is sitting in the Manettes' garden with Lucie and her father, Mr Lorry and Darnay, and they note a rush of passing footsteps followed by a violent storm: Carton ruminates, "There is a great crowd coming one day into our lives".

Some time later he finds Lucie on her own and tells her with tears in his eyes that in his dissolute life she is the last dream of his soul and "that for you and for any dear to you, I would do anything … embrace any sacrifice". He makes a rather similar offer of close friendship to Darnay, who, somehat bemused, accepts.

In 1792, with Darnay in prison, Carton comes to Paris and, stopping at the Defarge wineshop, the owners also note how much he looks like Darnay.

When Darnay is sentenced to die on the morrow Carton, knowing what he is about to do, gives specific orders to the Manette party on when and how to depart for London the next day. He induces the spy Barsad, of whom he knows enough to have him seized, and who is now a turnkey, to let him into Darnay's cell. Just before execution time, Carton slips in, he and Darnay exchange clothes, he takes Darnay's place and leaves Darnay to join his family and head for safety. An hour later Carton goes to the guillotine: "It is a far, far better thing that I do than I have ever done, it is a far, far better rest that I go to than I have ever known."

★★★DARNAY, CHARLES (Bk 2, II), personable dark-eyed man of about 25 dressed in sober black with hair tied in a ribbon, accused at the Old Bailey in 1780 of passing army information to the French. Also in court is a junior barrister to whom Darnay passes a note for Lucie Manette and it is generally noticed that this man, Sydney Carton, has a remarkable resemblance to Darnay. The trial ends in acquittal; afterwards Carton entertains Darnay to dinner in a tavern in Fleet Street. Carton drinks heavily and his guest wonders "at this Double of coarse deportment".

Darnay goes to France to see his uncle, a marquis, and tells him that he prefers to stay and work in England, renouncing not just his title but the estates to which he is heir as "a wilderness of misery and ruin".

In England he develops a career as a tutor in French and French literature. When he asks Manette for permission to marry Lucie and tells him that he is now legally has another name (as the noble uncle is dead) which he wants to tell him about, Manette says not to do so until the morning of the marriage. What he then reveals distresses Manette greatly.

In 1792, with the revolution full swing, Darnay in London gets a letter from the land agent Gabelle on the family estate, who has been seized and thrown into prison: the man appeals to "Monsieur the Heretofore Marquis" to come and save him from death. Darnay has never told anyone in England that he inherited his uncle's title but feels honour-bound to go to Paris and help a loyal servant.

He heads for France and is soon taken prisoner as "emigrant Evrémonde". In Paris one of his guards is Defarge, who says he will do nothing to help him. Darnay is thrown into La Force prison. Manette comes to help set him free but the public mood is against release and Darnay is there for 15 months while the Terror sweeps Paris.

When finally tried, he is acquitted because of the evidence from his father-in-law but is rearrested hours later and publicly denounced by Defarge, who at the tribunal reads Manette's own account of a marquis's misdeeds and his curse on the family: Darnay is sentenced to death.

An hour before he is due to be taken away, Carton slips into his cell and enjoins silence: the two men exchange cloaks, cravats and boots. Carton talks Darnay's place while Darnay, mistaken for Carton, reaches his family and heads for England and future happiness: he and Lucy will one day have a son who bears Carton's name – and who will distinguish himself in the law.

★★★**DEFARGE, ERNEST (Bk 1, V)**, aged about 30 in 1775, keeps a wineshop in the Saint Antoine slum in Paris. Doctor Manette has since his release from his dungeon been sheltered in a garret behind the wineshop. Defarge takes Lorry and Lucy up to see Manette and they take him to England.

Years pass. Defarge comes out to comfort his neighbour Gaspard, distraught at the death of his child under the wheels of a nobleman's passing coach. The marquis throws a gold coin into the gutter; it is thrown back at him.

Some time later a road mender from the region of the marquis's estate comes to tell the men in Defarge's wineshop how the father of the dead child was caught and publicly hanged in the local village. Defarge reveals that what his wife is always so busy knitting is in fact a register with a list of names in code – of those to be avenged.

Shortly afterwards, the spy John Barsad reveals in the wineshop that Lucie Manette is to marry Charles Darnay. Defarge drily comments: "I hope for her sake that Destiny will keep her husband out of France."

On July 14 1789 Defarge leads a mob from his wineshop and helps to invade the Bastille. Once inside he forces a turnkey to lead him to cell One Hundred and Five North Tower and there sees for himself the initials "A.M." and the inscription "a poor physician". From a wall he pulls a hidden document and keeps it safe. He gets Darnay rearrested and at the tribunal produces the document, in it Manette tells of a nobleman named "St. E." seducing a country girl and murdering her brother and the young physician from Beauvais being sent to the Bastille for exposing it; his account ends with a curse on the family. Darnay is sentenced to death.

DEFARGE, THÉRÈSE (Bk 1, V), sits behind the counter in her husband's wineshop always knitting and keeping check on who comes and goes. Also aged about 30 in 1775, stout and with a very composed manner.

Madame, silently and still knitting, notes the accident in which a child is run over by an aristocrat's coach, and looks steadily at its owner, the marquis. Her ceaseless knitting is a register, in her own code and symbols, noting "those who are doomed to destruction". Into the register goes the family of the dead marquis, "the children and all the race".

Years pass. On 14 July 1789, with knife in hand, she fiercely leads the women towards the Bastille.

She denounces Darnay at his second trial and having seen him sentenced goes to Lucie's flat to draw her in as well. Lucie has already left Paris but Miss Pross guesses the Frenchwoman's motive and tangles with her. Madame Defarge's revolver goes off, and she drops dead.

EVRÉMONDE, MARQUIS ST. (Bk 2, VII) (referred in the narrative only as Monsieur the Marquis), is travelling to his country estates when a child is killed as his coach is driven recklessly through the streets. He throws a coin at the distressed father and continues his journey, not knowing a stalker is clinging to the underside of the coach. Arriving at his estate, he meets his nephew Darnay from England and is contemptuous and dismayed when he is told that Darnay wants to renounce his estates and title.

The marquis retires. Next morning he is found in bed with a knife through his heart and a note: "Drive him fast to his tomb. This, from JACQUES."

LORRY, MR JARVIS (Bk 1, II), clerk in Tellson's Bank by Temple Bar, London, "steeped in bank business and its strongrooms", a bachelor of 60 with a healthy colour in his cheeks and a neat little wig, hides a compassionate nature under his businesslike manner.

The story begins in 1775 when Mr Lorry heads for Paris to bring back to England a onetime Tellson's client, Alexandre Manette, a doctor imprisoned without trial by the French authorities and newly released after 18 years.

He takes with him Manette's daughter Lucie and in a garret behind a wineshop owned by Ernest Defarge unites father and daughter and brings them to London.

He remains a friend and supporter throughout the years. In 1792, when he is 77, he leads the party – including Darnay, set free by Carton's sacrifice – from the chaos of Paris to safety in England.

★★★MANETTE, DR ALEXANDRE (Bk 1, VI), onetime

physician in Beauvais, thrown into the Bastille in Paris and "buried alive" until he knows himself only by his cell address, One Hundred and Five, North Tower. White-haired and weak, he is still disorientated after his release and finds comfort only in mending shoes. His bank friend Lorry gets him back to England.

Years pass. By 1780 Manette is settled in Soho, practising successfully as a doctor and living happily with his daughter Lucie, the past apparently just a shade. But when the French teacher Darnay comes to say that he wishes ro marry Lucie, Manette consents – and Lucie finds him once again at his shoemaker's bench.

On the morning of the marriage the father learns the truth about Darnay's identity. After the wedding he retires to his room and his shoemaker's bench, utterly withdrawn. After nine days he snaps out of it and goes to join the married couple while Lorry, with his consent, at last burns the bench.

In 1792 Darnay travels to Paris on a mercy mission. His family come after and Manette, with his record as a victim of the *ancien regime*, seeks to have Darnay freed, a process which as the public mood develops into the Terror takes him 15 months. When the case finally comes Manette's evidence sets Darnay free, but Manette is distressed when Darnay is immediately rearrested, all the more when at the second trial he finds it is his evidence that damns Darnay.

Carton's sacrifice frees Darnay: Manette leads his son-in-law and the rest of the family back to England.

MANETTE, LUCIE, (Bk 1, iV), blue eyes and fair-haired, travels from London with Lorry in 1775 to fetch her father, who always during his incarceration kept a few blonde hairs, which they now find match hers perfectly, but he is still too withdrawn to register the fact. Lucie is a ward of Tellson's after Lorry brought her to London following her father's arrest and the death of her English mother. She and Lorry take the father back.

When she faints at Darnay's treason trial in 1780 and is

comforted by her father, now in firmer health, she meets the barrister Carton.

The Manettes settle in Soho, where the doctor treats patients and she supports him lovingly. Love develops between her and Darnay. They are married and in due course have a daughter, Lucie, and a son who dies in infancy.

In 1792, having heard from Darnay that he has gone to Paris to rescue an employee in French custody, Lucie follows him with her father, daughter and Miss Pross. They are seen by Madame Defarge and when Lucie pleads with her for mercy meets with cold denial.

With Darnay freed after his second trial thanks to Carton's taking his place, she and the rest of the family leave Paris for freedom in London.

PROSS, MISS (Bk 2 VII), Lucie's nurse and companion since she was 10; she has red hair, a gaunt figure and a brusque exterior but is devoted to her "Ladybird".

In 1792 she accompanies her to Paris. When the family have finally left for safety in England she meets Madame Defarge, come in search of Lucie to rope in as another victim; Miss Pross struggles to block her, the woman's revolver goes off and she falls dead.

SELECTED
SHORT WORKS

For ease of reference, the roman numeral after a character indicates the chapter in which that character first appears.

THE CHIMES

Tragi-comic satire on inequality and injustice centred round experiences and dreams on a cold New Year's Eve of **TROTTY VEEK (I)**, elderly errand-boy who finds solace in chimes of the local church.

A CHRISTMAS CAROL

CRATCHIT, BOB (I), cowed and timid clerk badly treated in Scrooge's dingy counting – house, earning 15 shillings a week. On a cold Christmas Eve he goes to his Canning Town home and Tiny Tim.

CRATCHIT, TINY TIM (III), Bob Cratchit's youngest child, is a patient, sweet-natured little boy, under-developed, leg in irons, withered hand, his life feared for, cosseted by the family. He survives and gives the story its closing line: "God bless Us, Every One!"

SCROOGE, EBENEZER (I), "odious, stingy and unfeeling" elderly boss of a small counting-house, angrily dismisses Christmas as "humbug", sends his clerk Bob Cratchit home on Christmas Eve, begrudging him the next day off ("a day's wages for no work"). In his miserable lodging he is visited that night by spirits who show him his way of life is sterile, leaving him demoralised, humbled and terrified. Next morning, Christmas Day, he wakes quite reformed, "happy as a schoolboy", sends the Cratchits a big turkey, raises Bob's pay, shows generosity all round and becomes known as a man who "knows how to keep Christmas well".

THE CRICKET ON THE HEARTH

PEERYBINGLE, JOHN (I), jovial carter, adores his much younger wife, Dot, and is so devastated when he sees her embracing a strange man much more her own age that he contemplates murder, but is held back by the timely chirrup of a cricket on his hearth, which turns out to be the benevolent spirit of his home – and the stranger turns out to be Dot's childhood sweetheart, Edward Plummer, returned after long absence abroad to marry a friend of Dot's.

PLUMMER, BERTHA (I), doll's dressmaker: benevolent but blind (and therefore not as manipulative as her counterpart Jenny Wren in *Our Mutual Friend*).

THE ALL-DICKENS QUIZ: 50 QUESTIONS AND ANSWERS

In "Great Expectations", Pip believes his good fortune comes from Miss Havisham, but he's wrong. Who does it come from?

Magwitch

In "Tale of Two Cities", why does Sydney Carton go to the guillotine?

To save the husband of the woman, Lucy, he loves

Who is the banker in "Little Dorrit", fawned on by all but who came a cropper?

Mr Merdle

In "David Copperfield", who is always waiting for "something to turn up" to revive his fortunes?

Mr Micawber

In "A Christmas Carol", name Tiny Tim's father:

Bob Cratchit

In "Martin Chuzzlewit", who are Pecksniff's daughters?

Charity and Mercy

Who is young Martin Chuzzlewit's loyal friend, always cheerful when things go badly?

Mark Tapley

What does the architect Pecksniff steal from the young trainee architect Martin Chuzzlewit?

Design for a grammar school

"Martin Chuzzlewit": what does nurse Sairey Gamp keep in her teapot?

Liquor

Who's the pretty girl Nicholas Nickleby marries?

Madeline Bray

Who's the pretty girl Edwin Drood does not marry?

Rosa Bud

In "Nicholas Nickleby", what does the infant phenomenon do?

Ninette Crummles is a ballerina in her father Vincent's theatre group

How does Nicholas Nickleby take his leave from Wackford Squeers?

He thrashes him

Who is the mentally disabled teenager whom Nicholas Nickleby rescues at Dotheboys Hall?

Smike

In "Nicholas Nickleby", who is the dim-witted aristocrat who saves Kate Nickleby from prostitution?

Lord Frederick Verisopht

"Great Expectations": what's the relationship between the beautiful Estella and the convict Abel Magwitch?

He is her father

"Great Expectations": who is Pip's pompous and interfering uncle?

Pumblechook

"Great Expectations": who is Pip's kind friend who calls his much-revered father the Aged Parent?

City clerk John Wemmick

In "Oliver Twist", how does Bill Sikes die?

Accidentally hanged by a rope which slips round his neck as he is trying to escape

In "Oliver Twist", how does Bumble the beadle assess the suitability of his future wife?

By counting the number of her silver spoons

"David Copperfield": famous quote "Barkis is willin'". To do what?

To marry Peggotty

"Bleak House": how many men make Esther Summerson an offer of marriage?

Three (Guppy, Jarndyce, Woodcourt)

"Bleak House": what court case runs like a thread through the narrative, affecting the attitudes of many characters?

Jarndyce and Jarndyce

"Bleak House": which character disappears in a puff of smoke?

Shopkeeper Mr Krook, victim of spontaneous combustion

"Old Curiosity Shop": who forces Nell and her grandfather out of their shop and their livelihood?

Quilp

Because of what failing is Nellie's grandfather in such trouble?

He is a gambling addict

Who sues Mr Pickwick for breach of promise of marriage?

Mrs Bardell

In "Pickwick Papers", whose knowledge of London is "extensive and peculiar"?

Sam Weller

Which of Mr Pickwick's friends, boasting he's a sportsman, is hopeless at riding and skating and positively dangerous with a gun (he wounds Mr Tupman)?

Mr Winkle

What was Barnaby Rudge's pet and what was it called?

A raven called Grip

Name the pub with which "Barnaby Rudge" begins and ends.

The Maypole

"Our Mutual Friend": Dickens's own Jekyll–Hyde character: sombre schoolmaster by day and later violent psychopath. Who is he?

Bradley Headstone

"Our Mutual Friend": which Englishman regards the manners and customs of other nations a mistake?

Mr Podsnap

"Our Mutual Friend": which unlikely character saves that

Englishman's daughter from a ruinous marriage?

> *The confidence trickster Sophronia Lammle*

Vengeful ladies: Shakespeare gave us Lady Macbeth; who does Dickens give us, just as bad?

> *Madame Defarge ("Tale of Two Cities")*

Which novel is set entirely outside London in the industrial city of Coketown?

> *"Hard Times"*

What Dickens character personfies the ugly face of the industrial revolution?

> *Gradgrind in "Hard Times"*

Satirical picture of an industrialist in "Hard Times"?

> *Bounderby*

In "Little Dorrit", who is Father of the Marshalsea?

> *William Dorrit, father of Little Dorrit*

In "Little Dorrit", who is the grim woman in the wheelchair who seeks to control everything?

> *Mrs Clennam*

In "Little Dorrit" what great department of state is dedicated to blocking progress?

> *The Circumlocution Office*

"Dombey and Son": who is CEO in Dombey's office?

> *James Carker*

"Dombey and Son": who elopes with Edith Dombey?

> *James Carker*

"Dombey and Son": who falls under a railway train?

> *James Carker*

Name two characters who play music seriously:

> *Frederick Dorrit (clarinet) and Tom Pinch, "Martin Chuzzlewit" (organ)*

Name two Jewish characters:

> *Mr Riah in "Our Mutual Friend", Fagin in "Oliver Twist"*

"Bleak House": where, broadly speaking, is the coffee plantation for which Mrs Jellyby wants support?

> *Africa, banks of the Niger*

"Bleak House": when she abandons the coffee plantation, what is the next project she wants to support?

Votes for Women

Name two people using opium.

Captain Hawdon in"Bleak House" (he dies); John Jasper in "Edwin Drood" (fate not recorded)

Two skilled women who make clothing for dolls only?

Jenny Wren, "Our Mutual Friend", Bertha Plummer, "Cricket on the Hearth"

What was the last novel that Charles Dickens completed?

"Our Mutual Friend"